Jacques

Maritain

philosophe dans la cité /
A Philosopher in the World

La collection
Philosophica
publiée
sous le patronage
du département
de Philosophie
de l'Université d'Ottawa
est dirigée par
Guy Lafrance

The Philosophica
series
sponsored by
the Department
of Philosophy of the
University of Ottawa
is edited by
Guy Lafrance

φ PHILOSOPHICA
28

Jacques Maritain
philosophe dans la cité / A Philosopher in the World

Publié sous la direction de
Edited by   **JEAN-LOUIS ALLARD**

Éditions de l'Université d'Ottawa / University of Ottawa Press
1985

Vedette principale au titre:
  Jacques Maritain, philosophe dans la cité =
Jacques Maritain, a philosopher in the world

(Philosophica; 28)
Textes en français et en anglais.
Comprend des références bibliographiques.
ISBN 2-7603-1039-6

1. Maritain, Jacques, 1882-1973 — Congrès.
I. Allard, Jean-Louis, 1926- II. Titre:
Jacques Maritain, a philosopher in the world.
III. Collection: Collection Philosophica;
no 28.

B2430.M34J33 1985   194   C85-090082-4F

Main entry under title:
  Jacques Maritain, philosophe dans la cité =
Jacques Maritain, a philosopher in the world

(Philosophica; 28)
Text in French and English.
Includes bibliographical references.
ISBN 2-7603-1039-6

1. Maritain, Jacques, 1882-1973—Congresses.
I. Allard, Jean-Louis, 1926- II. Title:
Jacques Maritain, a philosopher in the world.
III. Series: Collection Philosophica; no. 28.

B2430.M34J33 1985   194   C85-090082-4E

Imprimé et relié au Canada / Printed and bound in Canada

© Éditions de l'Université d'Ottawa / University of Ottawa Press,
Ottawa, Canada, 1985

ISBN 2-7603-1039-6

TABLE DES MATIÈRES

CONTENTS

VI

PHILOSOPHIE SOCIALE ET POLITIQUE
SOCIAL AND POLITICAL PHILOSOPHY

VII

L'HÉRITAGE MARITAINIEN
THE MARITAINIAN INHERITANCE

X

APPENDICES

Introduction

JEAN-LOUIS ALLARD
Université d'Ottawa

The present book could be entitled: *The Proceedings of the International Congress of Ottawa (October 6-9, 1982) on Jacques Maritain, a Philosopher in the World*. It is in fact a collection of papers contributed for this Congress by intellectuals and university professors of various countries on the occasion of the centenary of the birth of Jacques Maritain (1882-1973). It has been thought that the richness and the quality of these papers justify their publication.

We have grouped these papers into seven categories in order to give the reader a better idea of their contents. This publication is bilingual, which means that the texts are either in English or in French, each text being introduced by an abstract in the other language.

Il faut signaler ici la table ronde présidée par M. Rafael Caldera, président de l'Union parlementaire internationale, et portant sur « la gouvernabilité de la démocratie » qui marqua la dernière journée du congrès. Les membres d'une commission créée par l'Institut international Jacques Maritain, soit les professeurs A. Ardigo, L. Baeck, J. Leca, E. Palma, A. Pavan, R. Papini, L. Sabourin et J. Vandamme, ont pris part au débat en y présentant leur point de vue sur le problème de la démocratie. Le résultat des travaux de la commission ayant déjà fait l'objet d'une publication intitulée *La démocratie au-delà de la crise de la gouvernabilité* — Rome, Institut international Jacques Maritain (I.I.J.M.), 1982 — , nous y référons le lecteur.

Each contributor to this book deserves our gratitude. We would like also to express our gratitude to all those who have made possible the very organization of the Congress of Ottawa and the publication of this book, either by their encouragement, by their financial assistance, or by their direct involvement : The Holy Father Pope John Paul II, Mr. Amadou-Mahtar M'Bow, Director General of UNESCO, His Excellency the Right Honourable Edward Schreyer, Governor General of Canada, the Social Sciences and Humanities Research Council of Canada, DeRance Inc., the Venezuelan Maritain Association, the French Embassy in Ottawa, the Canadian Commission for UNESCO, the University of Ottawa, Saint Paul University, the Jacques Maritain International Institute and the Canadian Jacques Maritain Association which have jointly organized the Congress, and the members of the organizing Committee.

It is with a sense of duty that we add a few Appendices to this book, on matters related to the International Congress, as a tribute to those who have so kindly accepted the invitation to be members of the "Comité d'honneur" of the Congress, to address the members at the opening session and at the commemorative Mass.

Le congrès international Jacques Maritain dont nous publions les Actes a fait partie d'une série de rencontres semblables comprenant entre autres un congrès qui s'est tenu à l'Université Notre-Dame (Indiana, U.S.A.) en mai 1982, un autre qui a eu lieu à l'Université de Milan à la fin d'octobre et les deux colloques de la Maison de l'UNESCO (Paris, 13-17 décembre 1982) organisés respectivement par l.I.I.J.M. et par les Amis de Jacques Maritain de Paris.

Pourquoi commémorer ainsi le centenaire de la naissance d'un philosophe chrétien décédé en 1973? Tout simplement, nous semble-t-il, parce que sa vie et son œuvre ont une valeur exemplaire pour notre temps; les héros et les saints ne sont-ils pas, pour reprendre une expression de Bergson, les véritables éducateurs de l'humanité?

Maritain nous offre un exemple très contemporain d'un intellectuel chrétien « voué aux intérêts permanents de la sagesse » : de la sagesse révélée et de la sagesse philosophique, de la sagesse spéculative (ou mieux contemplative) et de la sagesse pratique. Il a été un philosophe attentif aux besoins de son temps, « une espèce de sourcier collant son oreille sur la terre pour entendre le bruit des sources cachées et des germinations invisibles », un philosophe dans la cité :

> Nul métaphysicien n'aura trouvé, dans la familiarité de l'éternel, le secret d'une familiarité plus parfaite dans son commerce intime avec les soucis quotidiens de son temps. [...] Littérature, art, science, éthique, politique nationale ou internationale, on ne voit aucun

domaine de la vie et de la pensée de son temps qu'il n'ait personnellement habité, exploré et reconnu jusqu'à l'extrême limite de ses frontières, lieux naturels d'une pensée attentive à « distinguer pour unir »[1].

Notre civilisation est en état de crise, nous redisent les grands penseurs de notre temps; cette crise se situe dans les profondeurs de l'humain et est caractérisée par l'absence d'une philosophie de la vie qui permettrait aux hommes et aux femmes de comprendre les raisons qu'ils ont de vivre. Sait-on ce que c'est que d'être une personne humaine?

Il se pourrait qu'au milieu des conflits et des incertitudes de notre temps, Maritain puisse apporter une contribution appréciable à la nécessaire et incessante redécouverte des valeurs de la personne, des valeurs de la vérité et de la liberté. C'est notre conviction profonde que Maritain, un peu à la façon d'un Socrate contemporain, peut nous aider à découvrir un certain nombre de choses qui nous permettent de mieux percevoir et de promouvoir notre propre dignité et celle de nos concitoyens, notamment le sens de la vérité dont la source fécondante est l'être dans ses multiples épiphanies et l'Être, et qui s'exprime, à partir de l'émerveillement initial, dans une diversité d'expériences cognitives (« distinguer pour unir »); le sens de la liberté dont les chemins sont ceux de la vérité et de l'amour, ceux de l'épanouissement des personnes et de la responsabilité sociale; le sens du dialogue qui est à la fois don et accueil; le sens de la démocratie qui est une organisation de libertés; le sens de la coopération entre personnes de croyances différentes dans la cité et entre les peuples. Sur ce dernier point, il faudrait relire le célèbre discours que Maritain a prononcé à Mexico, le 6 novembre 1947, à l'occasion de l'ouverture de la seconde conférence internationale de l'Unesco, discours intitulé « Les possibilités de coopération dans un monde divisé ».

À ces quelques aspects de l'œuvre de Maritain que nous venons d'évoquer, il convient d'ajouter le plus important, celui d'une vie axée sur la recherche de la sainteté. Le témoignage du père Yves Congar est, à cet égard, très éloquent :

> La grandeur de Jacques Maritain — et, avec lui, de Raïssa — est, je crois, surtout spirituelle. [...] Qui peut dire la vie de foi, de charité et d'oraison de Jacques et de Raïssa? [...] Je ne veux pas sous-estimer le penseur, surtout le penseur politique, le penseur de l'agir humain, celui des distinctions épistémologiques dans l'activité de l'esprit, mais je crois que le plus grand de Maritain est dans le rayonnement personnel d'une intelligence lucide habitée par l'amour de Dieu et habitant la prière[2].

Il existe plusieurs intellectuels et plusieurs groupes qui s'inspirent de Maritain, mais il faut également dire qu'il reste, pour un grand nombre, une source inconnue et parfois méconnue. Il est permis de souhaiter et d'espérer que, dans notre monde incertain, s'éveille de plus en plus un désir de sagesse,

1. E. GILSON, « Une sagesse rédemptrice », dans *Revue thomiste*, n° XLVII (numéro spécial consacré à Jacques Maritain), 1948, p. 4.
2. Y. CONGAR, « Souvenirs sur Jacques Maritain », dans *Notes et documents*, n° 27, avril-juin 1982, p. 7.

un désir de se laisser interpeller par les sages, parmi lesquels on trouverait certainement Jacques Maritain dont la pensée risquerait de devenir impertinente à force d'être pertinente. Puisse la publication de ce livre apporter une contribution si minime soit-elle, à l'accomplissement de cette noble tâche !

I

La physionomie spirituelle
A Spiritual Portrait

Maritain's Intellectual and Spiritual Life: His Major Intuitions

RALPH MCINERNY
University of Notre Dame

La Vie d'oraison *et les deux livres que Raïssa a écrits sur leur jeunesse et leurs amis nous donnent une idée de la manière dont la vie de Jacques Maritain comme philosophe était enracinée dans sa vie spirituelle. Grâce à la publication du* Journal de Raïssa *et du* Carnet de notes *de Jacques, grâce aussi au compte rendu qu'on y trouve du* Cercle d'études thomistes *et à la publication de la constitution du cercle, nous avons encore plus de raisons de penser que la vie de Maritain fut inspirée par l'adage (modifié)* primum orare, deinde philosophari.

Ce fait trouve sa formulation théorique dans Les degrés du savoir. *Cet ouvrage de Maritain, peut-être le chef d'œuvre du thomisme au* XXe *siècle, nous fait passer de la philosophie de la nature et de la métaphysique à la théologie et finalement à la sagesse qui est un don du Saint Esprit. Nous trouvons ici l'unification de la vie spirituelle et de la vie intellectuelle qui reflète bien les perspectives de* La vie d'oraison *et du* Cercle d'études thomistes.

It may seem paradoxical that philosophy, taken as the theoretical use of our reason aimed at conceptual clarification and cogent argument, both utterly impersonal, should nonetheless, in its concrete role in human culture, bear the indelible stamp of the philosopher himself. It would be a peculiar argument that depended for its validity on the fact that so-and-so formulated it, as if *ipse dixit* were one of its premises. However, if authority is the weakest argument in philosophy, it is nevertheless undeniable that some philosophers speak with an authority that transcends the content of what they say taken simply as such. For well over half a century, Jacques Maritain's voice was one to which others attended, giving ear to what was said at least at the outset *because* of the person saying it. Reflecting on why this was so in his case turns out to be a good way of drawing attention to the nature of this achievement and the character of his contribution.

What strikes one about Jacques Maritain, what to a great degree explains the enormous influence he had, and has, is the fusion in him of the intellectual and spiritual lives. He did not view the cultivation of his mind as a pursuit which was separate, however much it might be distinct, from the more existential task of becoming what he was called to be. In order to see this, we must look into his biography but, at the same time, he provided us with an account, on a somewhat theoretical level, of this fusion and of the need for it.

I believe that it is out of this immersion of his intellectual life the pursuit of sanctity that Maritain's lively sense of the variety, yet interrelatedness, of uses of the mind arose. He insisted on the analogical diversity of cultural activities and that of course meant that there was both plurality and unity. *Les degrés du savoir* is the basic reference for this concept, but it must be supplemented by several later works. *Sapientis est ordinare*. Maritain's far-ranging interests were not the diversionary pursuits of the dilettante. In appreciating the distinctiveness of science and metaphysics, ethics and poetry, dogmatic and mystical theology, Maritain saw as well the way in which they all hang together as so many modalities of man's vocation.

How radically the vitality of the Church prior to Vatican II seems to swing around the great converts to the faith! One thinks of Dorothy Day, Chesterton, Thomas Merton, and it is as if they form part of a line that goes back to Newman and includes Gerard Manley Hopkins as well. In the France of this century, Jacques Maritain is surely one of the chief converts to the faith. Who has not felt privy to the inner lives of Jacques and Raïssa in reading

Les grandes amitiés and *Les aventures de la Grâce?* Now these can be supplemented by the *Journal de Raïssa* and Jacques own *Carnet de notes*. Why is the recently published correspondence with Julien Green just the sort of epistolary exchange we should expect from the man we meet in Raïssa's memoirs? The answer to that and the simplest description of Jacques Maritain is: a man striving for sanctity.

The young couple who turned away from suicide after seriously considering it were not moved by *joie de vivre* or only a return of animal good spirits. They were reconciled to life only when they could accept it as a gift from a loving creator. How improbable a means of their conversion Léon Bloy seems and yet, in God's providence, he was precisely the one to lead these young people to the faith, to become their godfather, to burn into their hearts the simple truth of *La femme pauvre*: there is but one tragedy, not to be a saint. No one could imagine Bloy tossing that off as a literary remark. It summed up his own deepest conviction. No one can understand Jacques Maritain who does not see that his overriding concern was to achieve union with God.

In recent years the connection between a person's being a philosopher and being a Catholic is thought of as accidental at best: these just happen to be true of the same person. Not only might it be thought strange to suggest that the connection is more than merely contingent, even Catholic philosophers seem to have accepted the view that philosophy is indifferent, even hostile, to religious belief. At philosophical conventions, one senses that not altogether unstated conviction that the serious use of the mind puts religious belief into jeopardy. A Catholic who lives professionally in this atmosphere can lead a schizophrenic existence. Worse, he may adopt an implicit fideism, the very antithesis of the Catholic view on the relation between faith and reason.

One of the great attractions of Maritain to people of my generation was his serene confidence that religious faith enhances and strengthens the pursuit of even natural truths: *philosophandum in fide*, in the phrase of John of St. Thomas that Maritain adopted as a kind of motto. The Catholic should not do philosophy sheepishly, as if, unlike everyone else's, his mind is not a blank slate and he unwilling to follow the argument wherever it goes. A programmatic skepticism has come to be regarded as an integral part of the philosophical enterprise, as if one could scarcely engage in it if he has antecedent convictions, particularly if these convictions are a result of the grace of faith. How terrible for the believer to accept the suggestion that his faith is an irrational prejudice. Jacques Maritain was there to remind us that faith is an all but practical *necessity* if we are to achieve with sureness vital truths accessible in principle to natural reason.

Who could look at the history of philosophy and conclude that all is right with the human mind, particularly when of late that history so largely consists of claims that all of a philosopher's predecesors have been in error? The thought of the Middle Ages, so airily dismissed by a Bertrand Russell, for example, when examined in its own setting and without the prejudices of the supposedly unprejudiced philosopher, can seem a high point in the history of western thought rather than an aberrant episode. In spite of this fact, we should not think Jacques Maritain was turning toward the past when be turned to St. Thomas Aquinas.

Actually it seems to have been Raïssa who first began to read Thomas and she read him as she read Albertus Magnus, in continuity with her effort to make progress in prayer. *La vie d'oraison*, the little work co-authored by Jacques and Raïssa, is called in English *Prayer and Intelligence*. This work embodies the point I wish to make. The Maritains saw the need for prayer if one were to pursue the intellectual life. This need was not simply that of the priest or religious. The Maritains were addressing themselves to the lay intellectual. They were actually saying that there is an essential connection between prayerful union with God and the effort to arrive at the good of the mind, namely, truth. Nothing could seem more remote from the conception of the philosophical life now regnant. Yet this insistence is actually a return to the great tradition in philosophy reaching back through the medieval and patristic periods into classical Greek philosophy. Think of the *Phaedo*, think of the *Protrepticus*, think of the *Consolation of Philosophy* and the *De modo studendi*. The virtuous life is a necessary but not sufficient condition for the successful theoretical use of the mind. Indeed, there are moral virtues peculiar to the intellectual life. Philosophizing is a vocation, not a career.

We know that Maritain decided against an academic career as a philosopher—though fortunately for us all he was not wholly to escape the "poison ivy" of our walls. We know that he and his wife took a vow to live together, as brother and sister, foregoing the hope of progeny the better to devote themselves to the pursuit of sanctity. The *Journal de Raïssa* gives us an insight into the prayer life to which both the Maritains devoted themselves, from their conversion (1906) until the First World War. In 1914, as Jacques notes in Chapter V of the *Carnet de notes*, began those meetings at Meudon which would eventually take shape as the *Cercle d'études thomistes*. The amount of space devoted to the Cercle in the *Carnet de notes* (pp. 183-254, plus the appendix pp. 393-405) indicates how large it loomed in Maritain's mind, both at the time the Cercle flourished and later when he was preparing his notebooks for publication.

In an entry for April 29, 1921, he wrote of the purpose of the Cercle:

Pour aider les laïques à maintenir la pureté du thomisme et à le répandre. Il faudrait que les membres se déclarent résolus à se guider sur saint Thomas avec une entière fidélité, à lire la Somme une demi-heure par jour au moins, à faire au moins une demi-heure d'oraison par jour. (p. 191)

Study and prayer. The two were to go hand in hand, nor was the prayer to be thought of as merely a pious addendum: it was essential to Maritain's conception of the intellectual life. To underscore this, there was an annual retreat for members of the *cercles thomistes*. These retreats continued until the outbreak of war and Maritain tells us that it was the war which effectively put an end to the *Cercle d'études*. He goes on:

Je voudrais insister un peu sur l'un des caractères les plus typiques de nos cercles thomistes, à savoir cette étroite union de la vie intellectuelle et de la vie spirituelle dont le garant était le vœu d'oraison. « Par là, comme il était dit dans nos statuts, ce groupement de séculiers et de laïques » avait « à la base de son activité un don de soi-même à Dieu très intime et très profond, » et offrait « aux âmes qui aspirent à la perfection tout en restant dans le monde un secours très réel, sans cependant entreprendre en rien sur la liberté de chacun, puisque le vœu d'oraison ne concerne que les rapports absolument personnels de Dieu et de l'âme. » (p. 235)

The statutes referred to are given in their entirety in the appendix.

It is surprising to think of Jacques Maritain as a great organizer and indeed in his retrospective remarks on the *cercles thomistes* he insists on the *point* of the organizing rather than the organization itself. The point is to put the lay intellectual squarely into line with the evangelizing task which falls chiefly on the shoulders of bishops and clergy.

One is struck by the fact that when the Maritains became Catholics they intended that everything they should subsequently do must come into line with that principal fact about their lives. There could be no question of a few pious practices juxtaposed with professional activity, a professorial career like any other but with Mass on Sundays. No, the Maritains became daily communicants, they conjoined their prayerful union with the Truth and the more abstract and concrete intellectual pursuits of truth. To pray well and to understand well are distinct, but they are separate only at their peril.

Perhaps this is enough to suggest why we cannot think of Jacques Maritain's pursuit of sanctity as unrelated to his philosophical and theological work. Whether we read of Jacques and Raïssa in the first years of their Catholic lives devoting themselves to prayer as well as study, or go on to the origin and evolution of the *Cercle d'études*, or pursue them through the long story of their lives, there is a unified vision of the way all things work together to the chief end.

Not only is the pursuit of sanctity paramount in Maritain's own life, I think it is as well the single simplest explanation of the appeal he had for so many Catholics engaged in the various aspects of culture and the intellectual life—artists, theologians, poets, philosophers, novelists and contemplatives— Maritain put before us a version of the Catholic task which excited and stirred and strengthened the sense one had that the use of the mind is, after all, not the whole of life, be it ever so important. It was Claudel who said that ''Youth is not made for pleasure, but for heroism.'' This was a message Maritain too conveyed. In an era when doing philosophy had come to seem only a matter of winning arguments, it was nothing short of edifying to be reminded that it is rather an invitation to become wise. *O sapientia*, was the motto of the *Cercle d'études*, and it had been Raïssa's suggestion. But there are, of course, degrees of wisdom.

* * *

If it is the hundredth anniversary of the birth of Jacques Maritain, it is the fiftieth anniversary of the publication of *Les degrés du savoir*. This is, without a doubt, Maritain's masterpiece. He wrote a dozen other books which, taken as literary wholes, are better books, but their aim is less lofty and their scope much narrower. *Les degrés du savoir* has both the strengths and the flaws of a masterpiece, but the flaws bother us no more than do lapses by Tolstoy and Shakespeare. At the age of fifty, Jacques Maritain produced a work of genius, what may prove to be the masterwork of Neo-scholasticism or, to be more precise, of twentieth-century Thomism.

The intensity of Maritain's devotion to St. Thomas, noticeable in the statutes of the *Cercle d'études*, is best captured by his variation on the Pauline phrase: *Vae mihi si non thomistizavero*. The little *Introduction to Philosophy* Maritain wrote does not prepare the reader for the creative and extended Thomism that characterizes Maritain's other work. The *Introduction* was the first philosophical work I read, and I welcomed its schematic character, its definitions—in short, its scholastic tone. The book might give the impression that Maritain thought that things are pretty much the same in the twentieth century as they were in the thirteenth century or even in the fourteenth century B.C. This expectation might be intensified when one considers the profound dissatisfaction Maritain shows with modern thought. It would be a great mistake to think of *The Peasant of the Garonne* as the cranky work of an old man which is somehow out of continuity with his earlier writings. *Antimoderne*—the very title—is eloquent in that regard. Descartes, Luther, Rousseau, Hegel, Bergson, Heidegger, Husserl, the Positivists—Maritain sets his face definitively against main currents of modern thought. But this lack of sympathy with much of modern philosophy does not prevent Maritain from being extremely interested in the various aspects of culture nor from extending and developing his Thomism so that it becomes a more comprehensive and nuanced system than it was when he received it.

But before speaking of the extensions and prolongations and new applications Maritain made of the thought of Aquinas, we must draw attention to the fact that all this was preceded by a close and careful reading of the text. In the Jacques Maritain Center at the University of Notre Dame, we have Maritain's copy of the two-volume Marietti edition of Thomas's *Quaestio Disputata De Veritate*. There are marginalia on nearly every page and there are as well dozens of little slips of paper on which Maritain outlined and analyzed the arguments of the text. We may be sure than when he spoke of reading the Summa for at least a half hour every day, he had in mind a similarly exegetical and close poring over the text. When Maritain extends the thought of Thomas into areas undreamed of by his mentor, we can be certain that he is doing so on the basis of a prolonged meditation on the texts of the Master.

Turning now to *Les degrés du savoir,* let us recall its full title: *Distinguer pour unir ou Les degrés du savoir*. The preface alerts us to Maritain's intention:

Ceux qui consentiront à lire ces pages s'apercevront peut-être que tout en nous maintenant d'une façon rigoureuse dans la ligne formelle de la métaphysique de saint Thomas, et en rejetant toute espèce d'accommodement ou de diminution destinée à rendre le thomisme *acceptable* à des préjugés irrationnels, nous avons sur plusieurs points essayé de défricher du terrain, et de reculer les frontières de la synthèse thomiste. (p. xiv)

Characterizing Thomism as "une doctrine essentiellement progressive et assimilatrice," which explains its influence on so many different minds and cultures, Maritain prepares us for the remarkable synthesis to follow.

What I have tried to suggest in the first part of this paper, the effective fusion of the intellectual and spiritual lives in Maritain, is something the reader senses in the opening discussion on the *grandeur et misère de la métaphysique*. From the very outset it is clear that for Maritain, the aim of philosophy is wisdom and the point of wisdom is to know God. Metaphysics is an effort to know God. "Sa grandeur : elle est sagesse. Sa misère : elle est science humaine." (p. 3) There is as well, at the outset of this magisterial study, not much more than an aside, a comparison of the poet and the metaphysician (p. 5): intuition as compared with intellectual perception. And there is the observation that a metaphysics which models itself on the current state of the sciences is bound to wither and die: as examples he mentions Descartes, Spinoza and Kant. But if metaphysics is a wisdom, it is an unsatisfactory wisdom; it is not ultimate.

Voilà donc la misère de la métaphysique (et encore pourtant sa grandeur). Elle éveille le désir de l'union suprême, d'une possession spirituelle consommée dans l'ordre même de la réalité, et non seulement de l'idée. Elle ne peut pas la satisfaire. C'est une autre sagesse que nous prêchons, scandale pour les Juifs et démence pour les Grecs. Excédant tout humain effort, don de la grâce déifiante et des libres largesses de la Sagesse incréée, à son principe il y a l'*amour fou* de cette Sagesse pour chacun de nous, à son terme l'unité d'esprit avec elle. Seule y donne accès Jésus crucifié, le Médiateur élevé entre ciel et terre. (p. 15)

After this opening discussion no reader can fail to see that the volume in his hands is not a typical product of a contemporary lay philosopher. It is not simply that, in presenting and expanding the thought of St. Thomas, Maritain is taking into account that Thomas was a philosopher because he was a theologian and it is the latter function which is his principal one. That would imply that Maritain's achievement is simply to give an accurate historical narrative of what Thomas did. Far more than that is at issue here. Maritain at the outset of his study announces as intrinsically relevant for what *he* is doing the same religious faith as Saint Thomas'. He is not reporting what was true of Thomas's convictions about a wisdom beyond human wisdom: Maritain is testifying to his own acceptance of the wisdom that comes to us only through the mediation of Jesus Christ.

Just as the fusion of the intellectual and spiritual in his life attracted many to Maritain, so too at a level of theoretical communication his programmatic assumption that the truths one accepts on faith must be put into relation with naturally achieved truths appeals to a Catholic who has felt the depressing redefinition of the intellectual life in a mode Maritain would likely describe as Platonist. This is the later-day notion that the cultivation of the mind can be successfully pursued in abstraction from the larger moral and existential tasks of the human person.

It came as no surprise to me that Maritain, in *Existence and the Existent*, felt affinity with some aspects of the thought of Kierkegaard. Indeed, it seemed to me that Maritain almost alone among Thomists saw that the Kierkegaardian emphasis on existence was to make a moral rather than a metaphysical point.

The first part of *Les degrés du savoir* is concerned with degrees of rational knowing, that is, the achievements of unaided natural reason. Maritain discusses philosophy and experimental science, critical realism, philosophy of nature and metaphysics. Whatever else may be said of Maritain's effort to put together philosophy of nature in the traditional sense and experimental science, it is certainly one of the three major views formulated by Thomists in this century. Indeed, the other views were fashioned largely in reaction to Maritain's. Needless to say, Maritain's views on the nature of experimental science affect his views on the philosophy of nature, and vice versa. After his treatment of metaphysics, Maritain goes on to speak of *les degrés du savoir supra-rationnel*. Attend what he has to say of the *trois sagesses*.

Under the rubric "mystical experience and philosophy," Maritain speaks of the wisdom of natural theology, the wisdom which is the science of revealed mysteries, theology as such, and finally the wisdom which is the gift of the Holy Ghost.

* * *

Les degrés du savoir is a remarkable book, not simply for the range of its topics, but for the vision of unity which animates the discussion. Consider what it is Maritain is suggesting. From man's engagement in the experimental sciences, seen as distinct from, yet related to, the familiar progression through the levels of philosophy to metaphysics, there is a single *élan*, a love and pursuit of wisdom, the desire to know and be united with God. In metaphysics, considered as natural theology, we have as it were a first and inadequate wisdom. Philosophy stirs our desire for union with God as He is in Himself, but philosophy cannot satisfy that desire. Only thanks to the salvific action of Christ and the revelation of the mysteries of faith is there possible the wisdom, the theology, which reflects on those mysteries. But this is not the end. Beyond naturel theology and scholastic theology is mystical union.

We are all familiar with the range of Maritain's masterpiece. Perhaps we are *too* familiar with it, and do not appreciate as once we did the power of its unifying vision. All the various topics hang together; they form a hierarchical order which honors their distinction one from another but not their separation. In discussing theology in the sense of reasoned reflection on the mysteries, Maritain remarks almost casually that the theologican who does not have a deep spiritual life, who has not had some mystical experience, could not meaningfully discuss mysticism. This is not to say that the theologian is thereby engaged in the analysis of his own experience as his own. Far from it. Nor for that matter is Maritain confusing the efforts of a St. Thomas Aquinas with those of a St. John of the Cross. But he is insisting that the things he distinguishes in his book finally cohere and form an order which is a new version of the Thomistic synthesis.

Maritain could not have written his masterwork if he did not have a lively sense of the different modes of knowing. There are adumbrations in this work of other daring prolongations of the doctrines he had found in Thomas Aquinas.

a) His reflections on the distinction between the speculative and the practical, and in particular on the degrees of practical knowledge, lead on to his distinctive conception of moral philosophy adequately considered.

b) Of even greater importance is the justly famous way in which Maritain takes the conception of knowledge through *connaturality*, first encountered in St. Thomas, and elaborated by John of St. Thomas, applied in its original setting to moral knowledge and the knowledge of faith, and extends it to speak of poetic knowledge as a knowledge through connaturality.

I have argued elsewhere[1] recently that Maritain's extension of the concept of knowledge by affective connaturality to poetic knowledge may present us with one of the best instances of the way in which he finds new applications of the thought of Thomas and engages in a genuinely creative Thomism. The aesthetics of Maritain is a story in itself, in any case. Let us recognize that before Heidegger, Maritain was drawn to a fruitful comparison of the thinking of the poet and the thinking of the philosopher.

A more recent instance of the kind of attention to the variety of modes of knowing that seems to me to characterize Maritain's work is found in *Approches sans entraves*, Chap. XIII, "Le Tenant-Lieu de théologie chez les simples." Indeed, each of the chapters brought together under *Pour une épistémologie existentielle* show us a Maritain continuing to cast the widest possible net as a Catholic thinker, to include and compare and make complementary activities which others simply failed to think together in the same thought.

You may perhaps be surprised that I have not given a place of privilege to what Maritain has to say of the intuition of being. This is not because I share the views of those who charge Maritain with being insufficiently alive to the centrality of the distinction between essence and existence in Thomism. Allied with this criticism is a criticism of the attention and honor Maritain paid Aristotle and those great Thomistic commentators Cardinal Cajetan and John of St. Thomas. I sometimes think that Maritain's critics lack his own sure sense of the way in which philosophy must be grounded in the common certainties of mankind. I am not always clear what is being proposed when

---

1. Ralph McInerny, "Maritain and Poetic Knowledge," in *Renascence* (Marquette University Press), XXXIV, no. 4 (summer 1982), 203-214.

I am told that the real distinction between essence and existence lies at the very heart of the thought of St. Thomas Aquinas and that an understanding of it is presupposed for the understanding of anything else he has to say. Surely that cannot be true if, as seems clear from any attempt to explicate it, the real distinction is an exceedingly recherché affair. When Maritain speaks of the intuition of being, he is clearly not referring to some metaphysical achievement of an esoteric sort. Here again his approach seems to me to be reminiscent of Heidegger and manifestly more attractive if only because more intelligible.

Why is there anything at all rather than nothing? This Leibnitzean query is put to good use by Heidegger. Taken just by itself it may be seen to function as a recalling of the wonder and surprise which are the appropriate responses to the very existence of things, ourselves included. In ordinary workaday life, perhaps necessarily, we take things for granted. One crossing a street would be ill advised to fall into rapturous wonder over the existence of a tree whose branches arch over the intersection. But there are appropriate times, and when we are about to do metaphysics is one of them, when we do well to recapture our sense of the wonder of existent things. I have often thought that the premisses of the Tertia Via make similar demands and that it is possible to classify philosophers in terms of their response to the claim that not everything that exists can be like the things which are brought about as the effects of other caused things. A philosopher who has lost his sense of wonder will be puzzled as to why we cannot simply keep introducing things of that sort (effects) to explain other things of that sort. But the crucial move is to wonder why there should be *any* things of that sort.

*   *   *

The late writings of Maritain are, with few exceptions, theological in the narrow sense of the term: reasoned reflection on the mysteries of faith. If Thomas was a theologian who became a philosopher in order to be a better theologian, Jacques Maritain was a Catholic philosopher who was drawn into theology by the very logic of his understanding of what the intellectual life is. And the fact of the matter is, from a very early period Maritain, while recognizing the formal distinction between philosophy and theology, refused to permit them to be separate in his own life. One thinks of his contributions to the controversy over the concept of Christian philosophy. Like Edith Stein, in *Finite and Infinite Being*, and like his master, Maritain wants to present a synthesis which inevitably includes both philosophy and theology.

The insistence on the relevance of prayer for the intellectual life was an insistence on the existential setting in which thought takes place. To forget the real human condition, to forget that the philosopher is a man of flesh and bone, is to run the risk of becoming the comic figure of the practitioner of ''Pure Thought'' who was the object of Kierkegaard's mirth.

To call attention to the *personal* existential setting in which thinking occurs prepares for the emphasis on the *social* setting: *Le philosophe dans la cité.* This is not really an option. Contemplative withdrawal must be motivated by charity, and charity relates one to all men. The philosopher does not choose to be *dans la cité*, but he can choose the mode and degree of that involvement. Subsequent speakers will draw our attention to the various aspects of Maritain's own social and political involvement. I have taken my task to be to suggest, however inadequately, the way in which there is fundamental continuity between *La vie d'oraison* and *Humanisme intégral.*

Jacques Maritain — Julien Green : une grande amitié

JEAN-PIERRE PIRIOU
University of Georgia

The prostitution of the words "friend" and "friendship" in both English and French necessitates a redefinition of the terms. We consult Montaigne, Ralph Waldo Emerson, Cicero and Bacon to determine the original meaning of "friendship." We then study the relationship between Julien Green and Jacques Maritain to show succinctly that the friendship that binds the two is truly exceptional and merits the epithet "great."

Montaigne, Emerson, Cicero and Bacon all agree that friendship is a natural bond, based on a rare, deep, unique mutual caring. Friendship is, moreover, according to Cicero and Emerson, disinterested; it must not be based on need. It cannot be formed

*in haste and it must stand the test of time. In order for friendship
to survive, it must be nourished by truth and affection. Bacon
states that friendship provides a confidant, clarifies one's understanding, and continues after the death of one of the partners.
Often, in fact, absence strengthens friendship. It is not surprising,
then, that the greatest friendships are manifest in correspondences.*

*Their exchange of some 206 letters from 1926 to 1972 con-
stitutes the most striking testimony of the friendship which joins
Julien Green and Jacques Maritain.*

Dans son essai « De l'amitié », Montaigne écrit : « Au demeurant, ce
que nous appelons ordinairement amis et amitiés, ce ne sont qu'accointances
et familiarités nouées par quelque occasion ou commodité par le moyen de
laquelle nos âmes s'entretiennent[1] ». Quelque deux siècles et demi plus tard,
Ralph Waldo Emerson abondait dans ce sens et proclamait dans ses *Essays* :
« I hate the prostitution of the name of friendship to signify modish and
wordly alliances[2] ». Je ne pense pas qu'il existe, surtout à l'heure actuelle,
dans la langue française, comme d'ailleurs dans la langue anglaise, de termes
plus galvaudés que ceux d'ami et d'amitié, ou de *friend* et *friendship*. De
tout temps, la réussite s'est mesurée le plus souvent à l'ampleur des biens et
des richesses que l'on possède et au nombre d'amis que l'on a, ou du moins,
que l'on se targue d'avoir. En français, on ne distingue pas plus entre ami
et connaissance qu'on ne fait, en anglais, de différence entre *a friend* et *an
acquaintance*. Et pourtant, qu'y a-t-il de plus ironique que d'entendre quelqu'un
offrir de vous recommander à un de ses amis dont il ne parvient malheureusement
pas à se souvenir du nom? Mais, qui oserait avouer n'avoir que quelques
amis et beaucoup de connaissances sans prendre le risque de se faire mettre
au ban de la société? Ainsi, lorsqu'il s'avère indispensable d'indiquer que
l'on fait allusion à un ami et non à une connaissance, on se voit obligé de
qualifier l'ami en question en ayant recours à divers adjectifs. On se surprend
ainsi à parler de « véritable ami », de « vieil ami », de « bon ami, » ou de
« grand ami ».

Si j'ai choisi d'employer l'expression « grande amitié » pour évoquer
les liens qui unissent Julien Green à Jacques Maritain, c'est d'une part pour
indiquer d'emblée qu'il s'agit bien d'une amitié unique; mais c'est aussi pour
faire écho au titre que Julien Green m'a lui-même proposé de donner à l'édition
de sa correspondance avec Jacques Maritain que la librairie Plon a publiée

---

1. MONTAIGNE, *Essais, Œuvres complètes*, textes établis par Albert Thibaudet et Maurice
Rat, Paris, Gallimard, 1967, p. 186.
2. R.W. EMERSON, *Essays*, New York, The Modern Library, 1940, p. 234.

en 1979 et qui s'intitule : *Julien Green — Jacques Maritain : Une grande amitié; Correspondance 1926-1972*[3].

Puisque nous sommes partis de la prémisse que, dans la plupart des emplois que l'on en fait, le terme amitié ne revêt pas sa signification véritable, proposons-nous tout d'abord d'essayer d'en retrouver le sens original. Puis, à la lumière de la définition à laquelle nous aurons abouti, nous étudierons les relations que Julien Green a entretenues avec Jacques Maritain afin d'établir que c'est bien d'amitié dont il s'agit. Enfin, nous nous efforcerons de montrer de façon succincte que l'amitié qui unit ces deux hommes est véritablement exceptionnelle et mérite bien le qualificatif de grande amitié.

Bien qu'ayant quelques idées personnelles sur la définition qu'il conviendrait de donner de l'amitié, j'ai préféré, ainsi que je l'ai manifesté au début de cet exposé en citant Montaigne et Emerson, interroger quelques grands essayistes qui ont écrit sur le sujet avec autorité. Il va sans dire que l'on pourrait consulter avec profit un grand nombre d'écrivains, mais je me contenterai d'ajouter Cicéron et Bacon aux deux déjà mentionnés.

Qu'est-ce que l'amitié? Tous s'accordent pour reconnaître que c'est un lien qui unit deux êtres et que ce lien est basé sur un sentiment d'affection réciproque. Ce sentiment est profond; il est unique et il dépasse tout ce qu'un homme peut imaginer et tout ce à quoi il peut aspirer. Pour Emerson : « Friendship, like the immortality of the soul, is too good to be believed[4] ». Selon lui, très peu d'hommes en sont capables : « Friendship may be said to require natures so rare and costly, each so well tempered and so happily adapted, and withal so circumstanced that its satisfaction can very seldom be assured[5] ». Interrogé à son tour, Cicéron répond, de façon identique : « L'amitié n'est autre chose que l'accord sur toutes les choses humaines, accompagné de bienveillance et d'affection; et je crois bien que, la sagesse exceptée, rien de meilleur n'a été donné à l'homme par les dieux immortels[6] ». Cette idée que l'amitié ne peut être un sentiment contraint mais quelque chose de naturel et qui nous est donné est reprise par Emerson pour qui une expression d'un usage pourtant courant telle que *se faire des amis* n'aurait aucun sens car, expliquerait-il : « Friendship demands a religious treatment. We talk of choosing our friends, but friends are self-elected[7] ». Pour lui, l'idée de se chercher des amis est absurde : « My friends have come to me unsought. The great God gave them to me[8] ». Qui plus est, l'amitié ne peut être que désintéressée et ne doit en aucun cas être fondée sur le besoin. C'est ce qu'affirmait Cicéron

---

3. *Julien Green-Jacques Maritain, Une grande amitié : Correspondance (1926-1972)*, Paris, Plon, 1979.
4. R.W. EMERSON, *op. cit.*, p. 225.
5. *Ibid.*, pp. 230-231.
6. CICÉRON, *L'amitié*, texte établi et traduit par L. Laurand, Paris, Les Belles Lettres, 1968, p. 19.
7. R.W. EMERSON, *ibid.*, p. 232.
8. *Ibid.*, p. 224.

lorsqu'il déclarait : « C'est donc la nature, plutôt que le besoin, qui à mon avis, donne naissance à l'amitié; elle a pour origine une inclination de l'âme et un sentiment d'affection, non la pensée des avantages que l'on en retirera[9] ». Enfin, une amitié ne peut se nouer dans la hâte et elle doit être mise à l'épreuve du temps. « Let us buy our entrance to this guild by a long probation[10] », recommandait Emerson.

Une fois toutes ces conditions remplies et toutes ces précautions prises, on peut véritablement parler d'amitié, cette « alliance of two large formidable natures, mutually beheld, mutually feared, before yet they recognize the deep identity which, beneath these disparities unites them » ; ce lien ainsi créé devient alors « the solidest thing we know[11] ». Toutefois, si l'on ne veut pas que cette amitié faiblisse, il faut la cultiver. Elle se nourrit de deux principes sans lesquels elle ne peut survivre. Il s'agit en premier lieu de la vérité, principe sur lequel Cicéron et Emerson s'entendent. Celui-ci déclare : « A friend is a person with whom I may be sincere[12] », et celui-là affirme : « Dans l'amitié, rien n'est feint, rien n'est simulé, tout est vrai et volontaire[13] ». Le deuxième de ces principes, c'est l'affection, comme en témoigne Emerson pour qui « the other element of friendship is tenderness[14] ».

Si nous nous sommes référés à Emerson et à Cicéron pour ce qui était de définir l'amitié, c'est à Bacon que nous laisserons le soin de nous en exposer les propriétés. Selon lui,

> A principal fruit of friendship is the ease and discharge of the fulness and swellings of the heart, which passions of all kinds do cause and induce . . . no receipt openeth the heart, but a true friend; to whom you may unpart griefs, joys, fears, hopes, suspicions, counsels, and whatsoever lieth upon the heart to oppress it, in a kind of civil shrift or confusion[15].

En second lieu, l'amitié éclaire l'entendement :

> It maketh daylight in the understanding, out of darkness and confusion of thoughts. Neither is thus to be understood only a faithful counsel, which a man receiveth from his friends, but before you come to that, certain it is that whosoever hath his mind fraught with many thoughts, his wits and understanding do clarify and break up, in the communicating and discoursing with another . . . .[16]

Enfin, l'amitié survit à la mort de l'un des partenaires et celui qui reste se substitue à celui qui n'est plus pour en continuer l'œuvre :

---

9. CICÉRON, *ibid.*, p. 26.
10. R.W. EMERSON, *op. cit.*, p. 232.
11. *Ibid.*, p. 233.
12. *Ibid.*, p. 228.
13. CICÉRON, *op. cit.*, p. 26.
14. F. BACON, *Essays or Counsels Civil and Moral*, New York, Doubleday and Company Inc., p. 78.
15. *Ibid.*, p. 78.
16. *Ibid.*, p. 80.

> Men have their time, and die many times in desire of some things which they principally take to heart; the bestowing of a child, the finishing of a work, or the like. If a man have a true friend, he may rest almost secure that the care of those things will continue after him[17].

Si l'amitié est un sentiment qui ne s'éteint pas avec la disparition de l'un des associés, c'est la preuve que la présence physique n'est pas indispensable à son épanouissement et à sa perpétuation. Souvent même, l'absence renforce et fortifie l'amitié et, c'est bien des fois dans des lettres, au fil d'une correspondance, que se manifestent et s'expriment les plus grandes amitiés.

Les quelque deux cent six lettres que Julien Green et Jacques Maritain échangèrent de 1926 à 1972 constituent le plus beau témoignage de l'amitié qui les unit. Cette correspondance illustre de façon frappante la définition, les propriétés et les manifestations de l'amitié telles que nous venons de les exposer.

C'est en 1925 que l'amitié se noue entre ces deux hommes que dix-huit ans séparent; Jacques Maritain a quarante-trois ans, Julien Green n'en a que vingt-cinq. Si l'âge apparemment les éloigne, on trouve dans leur passé respectif bien des choses qui les rapprochent. Le fait le plus saillant étant sans doute qu'ils soient nés tous deux protestants et qu'ils se soient convertis au catholicisme, à des époques différentes bien sûr, mais dans des circonstances qui se ressemblent. Cela est important, car cela va nous permettre de fixer d'emblée la hauteur à laquelle les liens s'établissent. Jacques Maritain écrira :

> Tandis que les chemins du monde et de la gloire littéraire, où il se sentait poussé avec crainte et une espèce de désespoir attentif, s'ouvraient à Julien Green, notre amitié se nouait dans les régions de l'âme[18].

Ce sont aussi les « régions de l'âme » que Julien Green explore dans son *Pamphlet contre les Catholiques de France*, ce petit livre qu'il publia en 1924 et dont Maritain se plaît à écrire dans une lettre de 1944 : « Un livre que j'admire tant et qui est à l'origine de notre amitié[19] ». L'ayant lu, Maritain se mit en quête de découvrir qui se cachait derrière le pseudonyme de Théophile Delaporte, car

> mon admiration pour la dureté de ces beaux contours pascaliens enfermant je ne sais quel tremblement de détresse et le sentiment de me trouver soudain en face d'une âme exceptionnellement profonde me firent désirer de rencontrer l'auteur. Il aimait se dérober; je finis par le découvrir[20].

Julien Green, lui, ne pouvait s'imaginer qu'un philosophe catholique prît au sérieux ce qu'il avait écrit sur la religion.

---

17. *Ibid.*, p. 83.
18. J. Green, *Pamphlet contre les Catholiques de France, Préface de Jacques Maritain*, Paris, Plon, 1963, p. 9.
19. *Julien Green-Jacques Maritain, Une grande amitié : Correspondance (1926-1972), op. cit.*, p. 89.
20. J. Green, *op. cit.*, p. 9.

Cependant, n'oublions pas non plus que si, avec une cinquantaine d'années de recul, il est peut-être aisé de se pencher sur la vie des deux hommes et de conclure que leurs chemins ne pouvaient pas ne pas se croiser ; à l'époque de leur rencontre, en apparence peu de choses les rapprochaient. Julien Green commençait à s'interroger sur son catholicisme et la philosophie n'avait pour lui qu'un intérêt relatif. Il rappelle dans sa préface à l'édition de la correspondance que pendant bien longtemps il eut du mal à lire les ouvrages que Maritain publiait :

> Avec une gaucherie qui m'était naturelle, je déclarais à l'auteur d'*Antimoderne* que je ne comprenais rien à ses livres, à quoi il me répondit en souriant que cela ne l'empêcherait pas de me les envoyer tous au fur et à mesure de leur publication et que j'étais d'avance dispensé de les lire[21].

Par contre, dès le début, Maritain lut toujours avec attention ce que Green écrivait.

Que le *Pamphlet contre les Catholiques de France* se soit trouvé à la croisée des chemins des deux hommes n'est pas discutable, mais celui qui l'a placé là, c'est Dieu. Green et Maritain en sont convaincus et ils ne manquent jamais de lui rendre grâce pour ce don merveilleux qu'il leur a fait. Maritain termine par exemple une lettre de 1959 ainsi : « Béni soit Dieu de l'amitié qu'il a faite entre nous[22] ». Il ne cesse de s'en émerveiller et il fait part à Julien Green de son trouble : « Il y a cette merveille de l'amitié que Dieu a mise en votre âme pour ce pauvre homme que je suis, et penser à un tel système est bouleversant[23] ».

Cette amitié, nous la voyons grandir et s'approfondir au fil des lettres échangées. On constatera qu'au début, elles commencent par « Cher Monsieur » et se terminent par une formule de politesse courante. Très vite, on passe à « Cher Monsieur et ami », puis à « Cher ami » ; et puis, « Mon cher Julien » répond à « Mon cher Jacques », et enfin, « Mon très cher Julien », « Mon bien aimé Julien » renvoient à « Mon bien cher Jacques » et « Mon très cher Jacques ». Parallèlement, ils ne terminent jamais une lettre sans s'assurer d'une affection et d'une tendresse profondes. Leur correspondance constitue un échange permanent de témoignages d'affection et d'admiration mutuelle, mais admiration ne veut pas dire pour autant flatterie. Au contraire, leurs lettres ont un accent de sincérité qui ne saurait tromper. L'un comme l'autre, Green et Maritain sont trop épris de vérité pour feindre. Rappelons simplement cette lettre que Green écrivit à Maritain le lendemain d'une visite qu'il lui avait faite :

---

21. Julien Green-Jacques Maritain, Une grande amitié : Correspondance (1926-1972), *op. cit.*, p. 6.
22. *Ibid.*, p. 114.
23. *Ibid.*, p. 98.

> Vous ne saurez jamais à quel point j'ai été touché de la manière dont vous m'avez parlé hier soir, mais il y a quelque chose qui m'a beaucoup affligé, c'est que dans le courant de notre conversation je vous ai menti sur un point très précis[24].

En fait, l'incident n'était pas très grave. Julien Green à qui Maritain venait de demander s'il comptait vivre seul avait répondu oui alors que la vérité exigeait qu'il dise non. Maritain ne fut pas dupe, mais Green ne pouvait pas supporter l'idée qu'il puisse subsister le moindre doute et il écrivit à Maritain pour s'expliquer. Une fois la vérité rétablie, Green supplie Maritain de lui pardonner cette faute car, ajoute-t-il :

> Je croix que je peux dire que je ne mens jamais et il m'est très désagréable de penser que c'est à une des personnes que j'aime le plus au monde que j'ai caché la vérité, ne serait-ce qu'une seule fois[25].

Cette affection que Green et Maritain se prodiguent dans chaque lettre, nous savons qu'elle est sincère. Rien de ce qui a affecté l'un des deux, que ce soient joies ou peines, qu'il s'agisse d'événements majeurs ou d'incidents de moindre importance, n'a laissé l'autre indifférent, et ceci aussi bien dans leur vie privée que professionnelle. Que Green s'excuse de n'avoir pas écrit plus tôt parce qu'il était fatigué, Maritain s'en afflige. Que Maritain ne puisse s'arrêter à Paris lors d'un voyage à Kolbsheim à cause de son état de santé, Julien Green s'en inquiète. Bien entendu, douleur et peine s'intensifient lorsqu'un deuil frappe. Les lettres que Green écrit à la mort de Véra, la belle-sœur de Maritain et à la mort de Raïssa Maritain, ou celles que Maritain écrit lorsqu'il apprend le décès d'Éléonore, la sœur de Green, sont véritablement poignantes. Mais si la peine de l'un attriste l'autre, n'oublions pas non plus que la joie de l'un fait aussi le bonheur de l'autre. C'est encore Emerson qui écrivait :

> I must feel pride in my friend's accomplishments as if they were mine, and a property in his virtues. I feel as warmly when he is praised, as the lover when he hears applause of his engaged maiden[26].

Quel plus beau témoignage d'amitié et d'admiration Julien Green aurait-il pu donner à Jacques Maritain, quand celui-ci le félicita d'avoir reçu le Grand Prix National des Lettres, que de lui écrire : « Je puis vous dire maintenant, qu'une des raisons qui m'ont déterminé à accepter ce prix était que vous l'aviez eu avant moi[27] ».

Les critiques caractérisent souvent les rapports qui existent entre Green et Maritain comme de cadet à aîné, de disciple à maître, et même de pêcheur à saint. Il n'est pas question bien sûr de nier la différence d'âge qu'il y avait entre eux, ou le fait que Julien Green s'est souvent tourné vers Maritain pour lui demander conseil; il va même jusqu'à dire dans une lettre qu'il le considère

---

24. *Ibid.*, p. 134.
25. *Ibid.*, p. 134.
26. R.W. EMERSON, *op. cit.*, p. 225.
27. *Julien Green-Jacques Maritain, Une grande amitié : Correspondance (1926-1972)*, *op. cit.*, p. 175.

comme son directeur, mais je crois que de telles généralisations trahissent la nature de leur amitié.

S'il est indéniable que Green a trouvé Maritain à un moment où il avait besoin d'aide et que le désespoir d'une âme qui se cherchait ne pouvait laisser Maritain indifférent, celui-ci ne s'est jamais imposé. Green écrira d'ailleurs bien plus tard : « Maritain n'avait rien d'un convertisseur[28] ». Une fois le contact établi, si Green restait quelque temps sans se manifester, Maritain attendait, mais il évitait de le relancer. Le bien qu'il a fait à Green, ce fut de lui dire sans cesse qu'il l'aimait et qu'il priait pour lui, mais aussi de lui demander de prier pour lui. Ce qui me frappe à la lecture de leurs lettres, c'est la réciprocité et l'égalité sans lesquelles, je pense, l'amitié devient une forme de paternalisme. Leur amitié, elle, a porté des fruits que tous les deux ont récoltés. Ils se sont ouverts l'un à l'autre avec une confiance totale : une confiance aveugle qui a guidé Green dans les démêlés de son âme et qui l'a ramené au sein d'une église qu'il n'avait jamais vraiment quittée; et une confiance qui fait écrire à Maritain peu de temps après la mort de sa femme : « Si vous saviez ce que vous êtes pour moi, quel refuge[29] ! »

Ayant, j'espère, montré que l'amitié qui unit Julien Green et Jacques Maritain n'est pas un sentiment banal, je voudrais, avant de conclure, mettre l'accent sur ce qui le rend exceptionnel, sur ce qui en fait une « grande amitié ».

Cette amitié, elle a tout d'abord résisté à l'épreuve du temps; qu'elle dure depuis plus d'un demi-siècle témoigne de sa ferveur. Elle a résisté à la séparation et à l'absence, mais bien plus, elle a survécu à la mort de Jacques Maritain. Le lendemain du jour où Maritain mourut, Julien Green écrivit dans son *Journal* :

> Beaucoup pensé à Jacques. On ne comprend pas tout d'un coup les mauvaises nouvelles. Le cœur n'en veut pas. Il faut pourtant qu'elles voyagent jusqu'à lui, qui les refuse [...] Quand j'étais inquiet, ses yeux clairs se posaient sur moi, effaçant toute ombre. Nous croyions les mêmes choses, et avec cette simplicité angélique qui était la sienne, et cette courtoisie de grand seigneur, il arrivait à me faire comprendre des vérités difficiles comme s'il venait de les découvrir lui-même à l'instant. Ces pauvres phrases que j'écris ne peuvent rendre ma tristesse[30].

Son amitié pour Jacques Maritain, Julien Green a voulu la proclamer au monde en me permettant de publier les lettres qu'ils ont échangées. N'écrit-il pas lui-même dans une préface à la *Correspondance* :

> Si j'ai livré ses lettres au public, c'est qu'elles gardent un reflet de la lumière où je n'ai jamais cessé de le voir. Puisse-t-elle briller aux yeux d'un lecteur inconnu comme elle m'éclaire encore aujourd'hui dans le mirage de la mémoire[31].

---

28. *Ibid.*, p. 194.
29. *Ibid.*, p. 148.
30. J. GREEN, *Journal* X (1972-1976), Paris, Plon, 1976, p. 124.
31. *Julien Green-Jacques Maritain, Une grande amitié : Correspondance (1926-1972)*, *op. cit.*, p. 8.

Ces quelque deux cent six lettres, auxquelles s'ajoutent vingt et une lettres retrouvées depuis la parution de la *Correspondance* et publiées dans le numéro un des *Cahiers Jacques Maritain*[32], projettent un éclairage nouveau et beaucoup plus intime sur une amitié exceptionnelle dont personne ne doutait, mais dont le journal de Raïssa Maritain, les écrits de Jacques Maritain et le journal de Julien Green n'avaient pas encore révélé toute la profondeur.

En concluant, je voudrais revenir à Emerson et je crois qu'il ne fait aucun doute que l'amitié de Julien Green et de Jacques Maritain confirme bien que : « The essence of friendship is entireness, a total magnanimity and trust[33] ».

---

32. J. GREEN, « Lettres inédites à Jacques Maritain », *Cahiers Jacques Maritain*, n° 1, septembre 1980, pp. 37-56.
33. R.W. EMERSON, *op. cit.*, p. 236.

II
Métaphysique et épistémologie
Metaphysics and Epistemology

The Christian Existentialism of Jacques Maritain

LEO SWEENEY, S.J.
Loyola University of Chicago

Maritain ne laisse planer aucun doute sur le fait que sa métaphysique est un existentialisme — authentique cependant, contrairement à l'existentialisme apocryphe de Sartre. Il est également clair qu'elle est un existentialisme théiste, puisque sa « méthode primordiale d'approche » de l'existence de Dieu (voir Approches de Dieu, *chap. 1) a la même source que sa métaphysique existentielle, à savoir l'« intuition naturelle de l'être ».*

Mais son existentialisme est-il explicitement chrétien? Il n'applique nulle part ce qualificatif à l'existentialisme, qu'il a élaboré d'abord dans le Court Traité de l'existence et de l'existant *(paru en 1947) et qui est ainsi postérieur de plus de dix ans à la publication, en 1933, de* La philosophie chrétienne. *Mais son interprétation de la philosophie en tant que chrétienne montre facilement les raisons pour lesquelles on peut appliquer validement l'adjectif à son existentialisme aussi, puisque ce dernier reçoit à la fois des corroborations subjectives et des données objectives de la foi et de la révélation. En d'autres termes, la foi en la révélation divine permet de connaître avec plus de facilité et une plus grande conviction que Dieu existe, qu'il est l'être subsistant, que son acte libre de création a pour effet de faire exister actuellement des choses qui n'existaient nullement auparavant, que l'essence d'aucune créature n'est son existence. Le dernier mot est évidemment au centre de tous ces aspects des choses : Dieu existe, il existe indépendamment de tout le reste, il fait exister toutes les créatures ; et toute créature existe par un acte d'être autre que ce qu'elle est. L'existence est aussi au centre de l'existentialisme authentique, cette position philosophique dans laquelle l'actualité a la primauté et « être réel » égale « exister » et provient d'une intuition de l'être dans des jugements d'existence. Par conséquent, l'existentialisme de Maritain est chrétien ; la foi chrétienne aide le connaissant humain à se rendre compte qu'être actuellement est suprêmement important pour tout existant, Créateur ou créature. Deux appendices suivent la communication : « Deux significations de l'existentialisme » et « L'intuition de l'être ».*

No one can doubt that Jacques Maritain considered himself to be an existentialist, and of a different sort from Sartre, de Beauvoir, etc.: his existentialism is authentic, theirs apocryphal.

> Let it be said right off that there are two fundamentally different ways of interpreting the word existentialism. One way is to affirm the primacy of existence, but as implying and preserving essences or natures and as manifesting the supreme victory of the intellect and of intelligibility. This is what I consider to be authentic existentialism. The other way is to affirm the primacy of existence, but as destroying or abolishing essences or natures and as manifesting the supreme defeat of the intellect and of intelligibility. This is what I consider to be apocryphal existentialism, the current kind which "no longer signifies anything at all."[1]

On the strength of that quotation one realizes that Maritain wanted his philosophical position to be taken as an authentic existentialism—i.e., a position in which "existence" (which means, for Maritain, the state of being

---

1.   *Existence and the Existent* (New York: Pantheon Books, 1948), p. 3; French original, *Court traité de l'existence et de l'existant* (Paris : Hartmann, 1947).

actual and not, as for apocryphal existentialists such as Sartre, Heidegger, etc., the state of being human) is given primacy,[2] in which "existence" confers reality because it bestows perfection, worthwhileness, significance upon whatever *is* perfect, worthwhile, significant. In short, it is a doctrine where "to be real" is "actually to exist."

Having granted, then, that his metaphysics is an existentialism, we may then ask, is it *theistic*? If the answer is rather obviously yes, an affirmative reply to the next question is not so evident: is it also *Christian*? But first let us reflect on the easier question: why Maritain's metaphysics is theistic.

THEISTIC EXISTENTIALISM

The reply to the question, is Maritain's existentialism theistic? is that his "primordial way of approach" to the existence of God has the same source as his existential metaphysics—namely, the "natural intuition of being."[3] Accordingly, let us preface our reflections on his existentialist theism by momentarily concentrating on this intuition of being.

Maritain gives his fullest and most detailed account of this intuition in one of his last articles: "Réflexions sur la nature blessée et sur l'intuition de l'être," *Revue Thomiste*, 68 (1968), 17-34.[4] But for our purposes let us see the simpler and briefer description given in the *Peasant of the Garonne*, the French original of which was published in 1966—just one year before he wrote "Réflexions."

After having disassociated his intuition of being from Bergson's and from "any kind whatsoever of charismatic intuition," Maritain describes it as follows. The intuition of being takes

> place in the heart of the most natural exercise of the intellect, and its only charisma is its *simplicity*—the mysterious simplicity of intellection. There is nothing simpler than to think *I am, I exist*, this blade of grass exists; this gesture of the hand, this captivating smile that the next instant will hurry away, *exist*; the world *exists*. The all-important thing is for such a perception to sink deeply enough within me that my awareness of it will strike me some day sharply enough (at times, violently) to stir and move my intellect up to that very world of preconscious activity, beyond any word or formula, and with no assignable boundaries, which nourishes everything within it. Such a descent to the very depths of the soul is doubtless something *given*, not *worked out*—given by the natural grace of the intellectual nature.
>
> And then, if luck should take a hand, and if the eye of consciousness, sufficiently accustomed to the half-light, should penetrate a little, like a thief, this limbo of the

---

2. For example, see M. Heidegger, "The Way Back Into the Ground of Metaphysics" in W. Kaufmann (ed.), *Existentialism From Dostoevsky to Sartre* (New York: Meridian Books, 1956), p. 214, quoted in Appendix One below, "Two Meanings of Existentialism."

3. *Approaches to God* (New York: Harper and Brothers, 1954), p. 3. French original: *Approches de Dieu* (Paris : Alsatia, 1953).

4. This paper was given first as a seminar on July 21, 1967 and is especially informative on how the intuition occurs psychologically. It is reprinted in the posthumously published book, *Approches sans entraves* (Paris : Payard, 1973) pp. 249-91. For an analysis of the paper see below, Appendix Two, "The Intuition of Being."

preconscious, it can come about that this simple *I am* will seem like a revelation in the night—a secret revelation which will awaken echoes and surprises on all sides and give a hint of the inexhaustible ampleness it permits one to attain. . . .

It is in a judgment (or in a preconscious act equivalent to an unformulated judgment), and in a judgment of existence, that the intellectual intuition of being occurs. The philosophical concept of the *actus essendi*, of the act of existence, will only come later. And the more profound and pure the intuition, the more accurate and comprehensive (barring accidents) will be the conceptualization of the various discoveries philosophy will be able to make by scrutinizing the real in the light of this absolutely fundamental principle.[5]

From that long excerpt, what can be gathered, first, on what the intuition of being is and, secondly, on how it grounds Maritain's existentialism? This intuition is an intellectual perception or awareness within a judgment of existence (''I exist,'' ''This blade of grass exists'') of the value of existence in an existent. It is a striking and deep revelation that the state of be-ing actual is supremely important and worthwhile for someone or something: it is that by which he or it is real, valuable, significant. Reflection upon that state of actuality, thus grasped, leads to the philosophical concept of the act of existing as the intrinsic cause or constituent whence flows that reality and value.

Furthermore, that natural although personal and spectacular awareness of actual existence as a fact and as a component in an existent leads to a philosophical position in which primacy is given to existence because it bestows perfection, worthwhileness, significance upon whatever *is* perfect, worthwhile, significant. In short, it results in a doctrine where ''to be real'' is ''to be actual.'' This is Maritain's authentic brand of existentialism.

Granted, then, that the intuition of being grounds his existentialism, why and how is it the basis of his theism? He addresses that point best, for our purposes, in *Approaches to God* (New York: Harper and Brothers, 1954), Chapter One: ''The Primordial Way of Approach: Natural or Prephilosophic Knowledge of God.''[6]

In this prephilosophic, natural and ''instinctive manner'' of knowing, ''everything depends on the natural intuition of being—on the intuition of that act of existing . . . in which all the intelligible structures of reality have their definitive actuation and which overflows in activity in every being and the intercommunication of all beings'' (p. 3). How does one achieve that intuition? By ceasing to live ''in dreams or in the magic of images and formulas, or words, of signs, and practical symbols,'' one is ''awakened to the reality of existence and of his own existence'' by really perceiving ''that formidable, sometimes elating, sometimes sickening or maddening fact *I exist*'' (pp. 3-4). Henceforth he is possessed by the intuition both of his own

---

5. *Peasant of the Garonne* (New York: Holt, Rinehart and Winston, 1968), p. 138; French original, *La paysan de la Garonne* (Paris : Desclée de Brouwer, 1966).
6. See above, n. 3, for data on French original.

existence and ''first and foremost of the existence of things.'' When this takes place,

> I suddenly realize that a given entity—man, mountain, tree—exists and exercises this sovereign activity *to be* in its own way, in an independence of *me* which is total, totally self-assertive and totally implacable. And at the same time I realize that *I* also exist, but as thrown back into my loneliness and frailty by this other existence by which things assert themselves and in which I have positively no part, to which I am exactly as naught. . . . My own existence . . . I feel to be fragile and menaced, exposed to destruction and death. Thus the primordial intuition of being is the intuition of the solidity and inexorability of existence; and, second, of the death and nothingness to which *my* existence is liable. And third, in the same flash of intuition, which is but my becoming aware of the intelligible value of being, I realize that this solid and inexorable existence, perceived in anything whatsoever, implies—I do not yet know in what form, perhaps in the things themselves, perhaps separately from them—some absolute, irrefragable existence, completely free from nothingness and death. These three leaps—by which the intellect moves first to actual existence as asserting itself independently of me; and then from this sheer objective existence to my own threatened existence; and finally from my existence spoiled with nothingness to absolute existence—are achieved within the same unique intuition, which philosophers would explain as the intuitive perception of the essentially analogical content of the first concept, the concept of Being. (p. 4)

A second stage follows immediately: a prompt, spontaneous and natural reasoning.

> I see first that my being is liable to death; and second, that it is dependent on the totality of nature, on the universal whole of which I am a part. I see that Being-with-nothingness, such as my own being, implies, in order that it should be, Being-without-nothingness— that absolute existence which I confusedly perceived from the beginning as involved in my primordial intuition of existence. But then the universal whole of which I am a part is itself Being-with-nothingness, by the very fact that I am a part of it. And from this it follows finally that since this universal whole does not exist by virtue of itself, it must be that Being-without-nothingness exists apart from it. There is another Whole—a separate one—another Being, transcendent and self-sufficient and unknown in itself and activating all beings, which is Being-without-nothingness, that is, self-subsisting Being, Being existing through itself. (p. 6)

This subsistent Being, is, of course, God.

But how is this primordial approach to God related to the traditional proofs of His existence? These latter (the five ways of Aquinas) ''are a development and an unfolding of this natural knowledge, raised to the level of scientific discussion and scientific certitude . . . and normally presuppose'' it. Before attempting the philosophic proofs, then, one must be ''alive to the primordial intuition of existence and conscious of the natural knowledge of God involved in this intuition'' (p. 11).

Accordingly, if both prephilosophic knowledge and philosophic proofs for God rely on this intuition, it is the foundation of Maritain's theism no less than of his existentialism.

A *CHRISTIAN* EXISTENTIALISM?

Finally, is Maritain's existentialism Christian? Nowhere (to my knowledge) has he applied the adjective to his existentialism, which he first elaborated in *Existence and the Existent*, the French original of which appeared in 1947.[7] But he had begun writing on Christian philosophy as early as 1931 for a conference which was given in December of that year at the University of Louvain and the essay was published in 1933.[8] This was further developed in *Science and Wisdom*, of which the French appeared in 1935.[9] Hence, his publications on authentic existentialism postdate those on Christian philosophy by more than a decade, and one can understand why he may have not have explicitly named his existentialism Christian.

But his interpretation of philosophy in general as Christian discloses why one may validly apply the adjective to his existentialism also. Properly intended, Christian philosophy is "philosophy itself [but] situated in the climate of explicit faith and of baptismal grace" (*SW*, p. 78). To explain: the *nature* of philosophy needs to be distinguished from its *state*. Considered in its pure nature or abstract essence, philosophy "is specified by an object naturally knowable to reason [and] depends only on the evidence and criteria of natural reason." But "taken concretely, in the sense of being a *habitus* . . . .existing in the human soul, philosophy is in a certain *state* [and] is either pre-Christian or Christian or a-Christian, which has a decisive influence on the way in which it exists or develops" (*ibid.*, p. 79). In Christian philosophy one receives subjective reinforcement from the "superior wisdoms, theological wisdom and infused wisdom, which rectify and purify in the soul the philosophical *habitus* with which they maintain a continuity not of essence but of movement and illumination, fortifying them in their proper order, and lifting them to higher levels" (*ibid.*, p. 80). Such reinforcement is exemplified in the ability faith gives a "philosopher who knows of the existence of God by purely natural means to adhere rationally to this truth with a sturdier grasp"; in the clarification and spiritualization the contemplative *habitus* contributes to the philosophic *habitus* (*CP*, p. 26); in the self-detachment and relief from ponderousness theology grants to a philosophy accepting its infraposition; in the freedom from futilities and opacities grace bestows on speculative intellects by its healing of nature (*ibid.*, pp. 27-28).[10]

But in addition to such subjective corroborations philosophy also receives from faith and revelation objective data

> which deals primarily with revealed truths of the natural order. The highest of these have been regularly missed or misstated by the great pagan philosophers. Moreover, these objective data are also concerned with the repercussions of truths of the supernatural order on philosophical reflexion. (*SW*. p. 80)

---

7. See above, n. 1, for data on French original.

8. *An Essay On Christian Philosophy* (hereafter *CP*), transl. E. H. Flannery (New York: Philosophical Library, 1955) p. ix French original, *De la philosophie chrétienne* (Paris, Desclée de Brouwer, 1933), p. 8.

9. *Science and Wisdom* (hereafter *SW*) (London: Geoffrey Bles, 1940); French original, *Science et sagesse* (Paris : Labergerie, 1935).

10. Also see *SW*. pp. 86 ff. *re* subjective reinforcements.

Instances of such data are creation, the human soul as object of salvation, God as subsistent love (*ibid.*, pp. 90-91), substance and accident, nature and person, essence and existence (*ibid.*, p. 102), God as subsistent Being, sin as an offense against God (*CP*, pp. 18-19). Accordingly,

> Christian philosophy is philosophy itself insofar as it is situated in those utterly distinctive conditions of existence and exercise into which Christianity has ushered the thinking subject, and as a result of which philosophy perceives certain objects and validly demonstrates certain propositions, which in any other circumstances would to a greater or lesser extent elude it. (*ibid.*, p. 30)

If we now apply his analysis of why philosophy in general is Christian to his conception of existentialism, we can readily see why the term is apt for the latter too.

Philosophy is Christian inasmuch as faith in divine revelation enables the reason more easily and with greater conviction to know (we shall attend only to the areas most relevant) that God exists, that He is subsistent Being, that His freely creating entails making things which previously in no way existed to now exist actually, that the essence of no creature is existence. The last word is, obviously, at the center of all those areas: God *exists*, He *exists independently* of all else, He causes all creatures *to exist*, every creature *exists* by an act of being other than what he is. But existence is also at the center of authentic existentialism—that philosophical position in which actuality has primacy and "to be real" equals "to exist" and which issues from an intuition of being within judgments of existence. Therefore, Maritain's existentialism is not only theistic (his primordial assent and technical arguments that God exists rest on the same intuition) but also Christian: Christian faith helps the human knower realize that actually to be is supremely important for every existent, whether Creator or creature.

CONCLUSION

Our aim has not been to praise or blame Maritain but to understand a position that is existential, theistic and Christian and, secondly, to offer data for reflection and discussion on an often controversial and always difficult notion: Christian philosophy.

All three dimensions of his doctrine are grounded on the intuition of being, which he illustrated always with this testimony from his beloved wife, Raïssa.

> It often happened that I experienced, through a sudden intuition, the reality of my being, of the profound, first principle that places me outside of nothingness. A powerful intuition, whose violence sometimes frightened me, and which has first given me the knowledge of a metaphysical absolute.[11]

Here his existential and Christian metaphysics began, and here my paper ends.

---

11.   Raïssa Maritain, *We Have Been Friends Together* (translation, 1942; French original, 1941), as quoted by Jacques Maritain, *The Peasant of the Garonne*, p. 111.

Appendix One

TWO MEANINGS OF EXISTENTIALISM

What does one mean by describing a philosopher as an "existentialist"? In order to answer, let us first ask what existentialism is. By force of the term itself "existentialism" indicates a philosophical position in which primacy is given to "existence," a position in which "existence" confers reality because it bestows perfection, worthwhileness, significance upon whatever *is* perfect, worthwhile, significant. In short, it is a doctrine where "to be real" is "to exist."

But what does "exist" mean? It can have at least two meanings. As used by Heidegger, Jaspers and Sartre, as well as by their European and American followers, it signifies: "to be human." As Heidegger explains:

> The being that exists is man. Man alone exists. Rocks are, but they do not exist. Trees are, but they do not exist. Horses are, but they do not exist. Angels are, but they do not exist. God is, but he does not exist. The proposition "man alone exists" does not mean by any means that man alone is . . . [an actual] being while all other beings are unreal and mere appearances or human ideas. The proposition "man exists" means: man is that being whose Being is distinguished by the open-standing standing-in in the unconcealedness of Being, from Being, in Being. (W. Kaufmann [ed.], *Existentialism from Dostoevsky to Sartre*, p. 214)

Or A. Dondeyne:

> Insofar as it serves to express the fundamental category, or more precisely, the "central-reference-point" of existential philosophy, the term "exist" no longer signifies . . . the simple fact of being [actual]; it means rather the manner of being which is proper to *man*. In this sense, only man "exists." Not that there is nothing outside man; man has, however, a mode of being called "existence" by which he is distinguished from all other beings that inhabit the universe. (*Contemporary European Thought* [Pittsburgh: Duquesne University, 1958] p. 29)

What, then, does "existence" signify in this its first usage? Not the state of being actual but the condition of being human. This is not to deny that things, as well as men, actually *are*—a fact which both Heidegger and Dondeyne emphasize. But it is an affirmation that only men, only subjects are real, in the sense of intrinsically and *per se* being valuable and significant, and that what makes them alone be real is the fact that they alone are *men*, they are *subjects*. Primacy is rooted in their subjectivity. This is the sense in which "existence" is understood when one calls Sartre, Heidegger, Marcel, etc. "existentialists." According to them men alone "exist" and this only while freely choosing. These philosophers give man primacy; they restrict reality to human subjects in their free decisions.

But "existence" can have another meaning—namely, the state of *being actual* rather than being merely intra-mental, fictional, imaginary. When predicated in this signification, "exists" expresses that the thing in question is extra-mental, it actually *is*. It is actually present outside nothingness. It possesses the status of be-ing rather than of nonbe-ing. If, then, "to exist" is "to be actual" and if "to be actual" primarily makes the existent real, then any actual existent, no matter what sort it may be, is real by the very fact that it actually exists. Reality is not restricted to any one kind of being, whether human, subhuman or, for that matter, superhuman, but extends as far as does actuality itself.

Are Sartre, Heidegger, Marcel, etc. existentialists in this sense? Obviously not. Although they are no longer idealists (as some of them were in the early stages of their intellectual life) and, thus, they grant that things actually are outside the mind, still reality for them is not centered in actuality. Granted that things do actually exist, none of them is real because they are actual. Some things (i.e., men in their free decisions) are real but only because they are men exercising their freedom. In short, only human existents are genuinely real, and they are this not because they are existent but because they are human. So speak Sartre, Heidegger, Marcel, etc.

Sartre's (and others') position is, then, at odds with the "existentialism" coming from the second meaning of "existence" (see two paragraphs above)— namely, the existentialism which gives primacy to actuality, in which actuality confers reality upon all actual things by bestowing upon them perfection, worthwhileness, significance. This is an existentialism which is authentically so and the other (that which gives primacy to be-ing man, to be-ing a subject) is an unauthentic existentialism. Accordingly, Sartre and others can be viewed as rejecting an authentic existentialism and espousing an unauthentic one. Why so?

The adjective "authentic" is intended to express that the item of which it is predicated is genuinely what its name indicates it should be and seems to be (e.g., "authentic freedom, love, religion": worthy of the name; versus phony, fraudulent, misleading, misnomer). But the meaning which "exists" (at least in English) spontaneously, ordinarily, immediately brings to mind is "actually is," "is actual" (e.g., "Life does exist in galaxies other than ours"; "That type of machine already does exist"; "Launching pads for intercontinental missiles actually do exist in Red China"; "Someone actually is downstairs now"; "There actually is a fire in the attic roof"). Therefore, when applied to existence, "authentic" emphasizes that "existence" in its spontaneous and straightforward sense precisely is the state of being actual. It focuses our attention upon the fact that an existing thing is an *actual* thing. It stresses that "to exist" is "to be actual" and not (say) "to be human," "to be free," "to be a subject." Hence, if "existence" is intended in these latter senses, it is used in an unauthentic way: existence no longer genuinely signifies what it seems to mean by the force of the term itself, since it no longer points to the state of *be-ing* but of being *human*. And a philosopher who gives primacy to existence in this unauthentic sense of "being a man," being a human subject" is pushing an existentialism which is unauthentic. And this, I suggest, is what Sartre, along with others, is doing. Because he gives primacy not to actuality but to human subjectivity, his philosophical position is a humanism, a philosophy of subjectivity or (in the case of Marcel) of intersubjectivity. It is not an existentialism except in an unauthentic sense.

Appendix Two

THE INTUITION OF BEING

In order to understand Maritain on the intuition of being, let us begin by listing some sentences (see above, Appendix One, last paragraph) to illustrate what existence ordinarily and spontaneously brings to mind.

"Life does exist in galaxies other than ours"

"Launching pads for intercontinental missiles actually do exist in China"

"Someone actually is downstairs now"

"There actually is a fire in the attic roof"

Although others may consider those propositions existential, Maritain views them as expressing copulative and not truly existential judgments. I say this in light of his last explanation of the intuition of being: "Réflexions sur la nature blessée et sur l'intuition de l'être," *Revue Thomiste*, 68 (1968), 17-34 (reprinted in *Approches sans entraves* [Paris: Fayard, 1973]). For example, in "Someone actually-is-downstairs-now" or "A fire actually-is-in-the-attic," the hyphenated words express a predicate applied to or coupled with the subject. One is on the level not of *Sein* but of *Dasein*, not of be-ing but of being-there. The concept of existence issuing from such judgments is known after the manner of an essence or of a quality. It is univocal. It is abstractive, it pertains to the first level of abstraction (*ibid.*, pp. 24-25 and passim).

In order to move from the level of *Dasein* to *Sein*, from univocity to analogy, from abstraction to contemplation, the human knower needs the intuition of being, within which there occurs a genuinely existential judgment ("I am," "This rose exists"), by reflection upon which he achieves a concept of existence which is analogous and not univocal, which is judicative and not abstractive in origin.

What does Maritain mean? We shall realize this if we ask, as he does: how does existence, found in the material things we perceive, become proportioned to the intelligence and spiritualized so that the intelligence can truly *see* it in and by its judgmental act? One must, Maritain answers, distinguish three stages in the process, the *first* of which is (say) my visual perception of this red rose. My eyes have received a sensible species or intentional form from the surface of the petals reflecting the light which acts on the physical organ of sight so that I can see the color and, simultaneously, the existence of the flower—this last "not by a species but by the intentional action exercised on the sense when receiving the species of the color of the rose" (pp. 20-

21) and thus existence would be a *sensible per accidens* (a point, however, which Maritain does not make).

In the *second* stage I know *that I see*, and this without needing the imagination or phantasms, since the intelligence is aware not only of the color of the rose but also of *seeing* that rose—i.e., of the cognitive activity of the external sense. That activity of seeing is, then, involved in a twofold intentional state: an awareness of its object (the *color* of the rose, intentionally received by the sense faculty through the sensible species) and an awareness of the *rose* (intentionally apprehended by the intelligence through an idea). Accompanying the seeing of the rose is its existence, rendered present in the sense by the intentional activity in receiving the sensible species and made present (implicitly, only) in the intellect by its being implicated in the rose (the object of an *intentio intellecta*) which the intellect knows that I see and which is-there. The intellect is then operating in the first degree of abstraction in saying, "That rose is-there," it is-present-to-me. This is the level of *Dasein* (p. 21), where *Sein* and existence, properly understood, are not present except in a hidden fashion, as implied in something else and without actual recognition yet by the intellect. The existence of the rose is already spiritualized but only potentially within another intelligible.

In the *third* stage the intellect, while the eye is seeing the red rose and it itself is affirming that the red rose is-there, moves to a higher level, which is not only that of the third degree of abstraction but also that of a natural contemplation in which thought escapes abstraction and where the light of the intuition of being suddenly shines forth. The *existence* of the rose is now grasped explicitly. It is actually spiritualized and actually proportioned to the intellect—not by a species or any *intentio intellecta* but by an *intentio intelligens* in a genuinely existential judgment (p. 22) that the red rose *exists, actually is*. Those verbs now have a fullness of metaphysical meaning, and being in the mystery of its limitless horizon and in its rich analogy discloses itself, even though like a rose (p. 23).

Such is, in substance, a paraphrase or translation of Maritain's reply to the question he had proposed earlier: how does existence, found in the material things we perceive, become proportioned to the intelligence and spiritualized so that the intelligence can truly see it within itself in and by an existential judgment (p. 20)? It is while the human intellect sees existence whithin such a judgment that the knower intuits being.

The Integral Humanism
of Jacques Maritain and the
Personalism of John Paul II

BERNARD A. GENDREAU
Xavier University, Cincinnati

Jacques Maritain et Jean-Paul II sont, tous deux, des penseurs personnalistes ayant une assise thomiste. Toutefois, leur méthode philosophique est différente et complémentaire. À l'accent métaphysique de Maritain correspond l'accent phénoménologique de Jean-Paul II.

D'une part, Maritain définit ainsi la personne humaine : un être psychosomatique doué d'une intelligence et d'une volonté libre, un agent spirituel et libre dont la société doit reconnaître la valeur en tant que personne. *D'autre part, Jean-Paul II voit* la personne *à travers l'expérience unique d'une conscience vécue*

*dans un agir qui prend place dans une situation existentielle; le
sujet humain, réalité métaphysique, devient un sujet humain dans
l'expérience de son agir.*

*Ainsi, Maritain, en toute fidélité à Thomas d'Aquin, utilise
une méthode qui se situe dans le cadre d'une philosophie de l'être,
alors que Jean-Paul II, ayant appris la philosophie à l'école de
Max Scheler, élabore sa pensée au moyen d'une analyse phénoménologique de la conscience de l'expérience vécue, au moyen
d'une approche réflexive, enrichissant ainsi son* thomisme *de la
méthode phénoménologique.*

*Dans cette communication, nous tentons de mettre en lumière
les raisons qui expliquent cette différence méthodologique de la
pensée de Jacques Maritain et de celle de Jean-Paul II, ainsi que
la complémentarité de leur contribution au personnalisme chrétien.*

1. PROBLEMATIQUE

Could there be a complementarity in the contribution to Christian Personalism of the philosophy of being of Jacques Maritain and the philosophy
of acting of John Paul II? Would the phenomenological elaborations of John
Paul II in bringing out a new way of thinking about the notion of person
enrich the metaphysical analysis of Maritain with regard to the person? Would
the speculative insights of Jacques Maritain in defending the classical way of
thinking of the notion of person serve to provide an understanding of the
ontological base John Paul II requires for his views on the person as the
human self brought out through consciousness in order to supplement the
understanding of the metaphysical human subject? Would the person-acting
of John Paul II depend on the foundation of the person-being and would
Maritain's person-being develop a new openness in the person-acting?

2. RELEVANCE AND RELATIONSHIP OF MARITAIN AND JOHN PAUL

John Paul II, in proclaiming his own allegiance to the philosophy of
Thomas Aquinas, singles out Maritain as the model of profound understanding
of Thomas Aquinas and of meaningful development relevant to our time
(November 17, 1979 speech commemorating Aeterni Patris, *Revue Thomiste*,
1980, pp. 7-8). There is a present-day interest in both Maritain and John Paul
II, perhaps especially outside the university. For Maritain, there is an American,
a Canadian, and an international association. These have been instrumental
in setting up congresses in honor of the centennial of Maritain's birth at Notre
Dame in May 1982 and in Ottawa, Canada in October. The international
association has an important research center in Italy and promotes many
seminars. The University of Notre Dame has the Maritain Institute. The

Maritain Center at Kolbsheim with its *Cercle d'études Jacques et Raïssa Maritain* and the Maritain archives produces the *Cahiers Jacques Maritain*. The International Institute J. Maritain publishes *Notes et documents*. The first volume of a 15-volume set of the complete works of Maritain has just come out. The works of John Paul have been published especially in *Analecta Husserliana* but also elsewhere, in North America and abroad, and new translations are in preparation for publication. Many writings on John Paul are coming out. The following works are relevant for our discussion: G. H. Williams, *The Mind of John Paul II, Origins of his Thought and Action*, New York: Seabury, 1981; Ronald D. Lawler, *The Christian Personalism of John Paul II*, Chicago Herald Press, 1980; Andrew N. Woznicki, *Karol Wojtyla's Existential Personalism: A Christian Humanism*, New Britain, Conn.: Mariel, 1980. And there is the American Catholic Philosophical Association (A.C.P.A.) Toronto meeting with its confrontation between A.T. Tymieniecka; "The Origins of the Philosophy of John Paul II," and A. Woznicki, "The Christian Humanism of Cardinal Karol Wojtyla" (A.C.P.A. Proceedings, 1979, pp. 16-27·. 28-35). Maritain still can rate an headline: *The Wanderer*, September 2, 1982, "Maritain, Personhood, and the State." The same newspaper carries the weekly Wednesday General Audiences on *The Theology of the Body*, which is said to represent a book as yet unpublished.

All of this is to indicate that both Maritain and John Paul II have a readership and an audience, which is at once critical and creative in the use of these two authors who present a personalism with a base in Thomistic thought, being developed in the context of the early and late twentieth-century intellectual crisis as it affects Christian philosophical thought. The philosophical methodologies found in the two are different and complementary. The metaphysical emphasis in Maritain counterbalances the phenomenological emphasis in John Paul II. They each add something special to the discussion. The presentation is made to celebrate the centennial of Maritain's birth in 1882 and to honor the contributions of our philosopher-pope, John Paul II (Karol Cardinal Wojtyla), elected in 1978. It would be fascinating to see the results if Catholic seminarians and college students carried copies of the works of Maritain and John Paul II along with their *Sein und Zeit, L'être et le néant,* and *Philosophical Investigations.*

3. TWO PHILOSOPHICAL PERSPECTIVES IN THE PHILOSOPHY OF PERSON

The philosophy of being in Maritain stands out in its mediaeval classical form with an emphasis on being as the center of the elaboration. The philosophy of acting in John Paul stands out in its contemporary structuralist form with an emphasis on consciousness at the center of the elaboration.

Person is defined by Maritain as a special kind of being already constituted in its nature and in its properties to serve as a base for the pursuit of perfection and completion. The person is a being which operates in a specific way inasmuch as it is endowed with intellect and will, it involves a body and a soul, and it has a specific finality. The individual substance of a rational nature subsisting in existence as a unique subject achieves completion in a unique way as a free and spiritual agent operating in an ensouled body with needs and goals which will be dealt with by the individual in society as a person with its own worth. All these aspects of the person are made clear in the philosophizing of Jacques Maritain.

Person is brought out according to John Paul through its own unique experience as a consciousness lived through in the acting taking place in the existential situation of a real world. The human subject as a metaphysically given reality becomes a human self in the experiencing of the self acting. The bringing out of the person or the bringing forth of the person depends on the conscious experience involved in the acting of the operating subject. The person appears successively in its own interior conscious lived dimension as self-determination, self-domination, self-possession, self-consciousness, self-fulfillment, with an open structure for its autoteleology leading to happiness in its authentic transcendence; the experimental fulfillment of the person as conscious human self becomes personal through the communal participation within a community of persons. The conscious act—as the root of human transcendence—implies going beyond the human subject within its metaphysical make-up, with its ontological acts, to bring about the human self with its conscious acting within a community of persons in a relationship of participation beyond the organization of mutual cooperation towards a common goal. The metaphysically oriented philosophy of being of Maritain develops through a speculative approach, giving an insight which identifies the person as a definite being, as a unique definite subject of perfective acts. The phenomenologically oriented philosophy of acting of John Paul II develops through a reflexive approach bringing out the consciousness, which experiences the person in its role as a center for acting, as a way to bring itself out in the open in its uniqueness.

4.   TWO PHILOSOPHICAL METHODOLOGIES IN THE PHILOSOPHY OF PERSON

Maritain, true to his commitment to Thomas Aquinas (Vae mihi si non thomistizavero), keeps his methodology within the framework of a philosophy of being, concentrating on the evidence of the object and on the intellectualist intuition of being, to achieve through abstraction, judgment, and demonstration an objective, true, certain and necessary knowledge of what the make-up of the person is and how it serves as a base for operating towards the person's own perfection as a being in the world and in society, and as a transcendent being having a nature and being a creature. The theoretical awareness of the being will give the truth that will make the person free. The kind of being the person is gives it its dignity and justifies its natural rights to the properly human goods it needs for its perfection. Classical mediaeval methodology is at the base of a rich development of insights about the person. John Paul, having learned to philosophize in the contemporary vein from Max Scheler, develops his methodology within the framework of a philosophy of acting, concentrating on the phenomenological analysis of the consciousness of the lived experience of the person acting, alive with the awareness of its action and of itself as agent. This reflexive approach to the human self as conscious subject of acting complements any reflecting approach to the human subject as reality with acts. Having rejected Scheler's phenomenological personalist ethics in 1953 as incompatible with a properly Catholic ethics, John Paul II still uses phenomenology for his own personalism twenty-five years or so later. John Paul II, in enriching his Thomism with the phenomenological method and insights, is following the long tradition of philosophizing Christians who, while holding on to the true doctrine of their thought and faith, use current methodologies to resolve new difficulties and to offer new opportunities, as is evidenced in Augustine with Neo-Platonism, Thomas Aquinas with Aristotelianism, Christian Woolff with Neo-Scholasticism, Kant with Maréchalian Transcendental Thomism. We should be grateful to have John Paul II as Karol Cardinal Wojtyla work out a new integrated, synthetic, and adequate personalism through the phenomenological method, with its base in Scheler and its realistic stance with Imgarden, complementing and developing the basic insights on Person of Thomas Aquinas. The negative attitude of Maritain towards modern and contemporary methodologies which appear to him to lead to a depreciating and avoiding of being as the central philosophical intuition, making of the thinkers using these methodologies ideosophers instead of ontosophers possessed of wisdom (*Antimoderne*, *The Paysan of the Garonne*), would preclude the use of phenomenology by Maritain to determine the meaning and value of person. The concern of John Paul II about the limitations and notion of person, when determined on the metaphysical level of a philosophy of being which leaves aside all the opportunity to bring out deeper and more meaningful aspects of the whole person, explains the fact that, instead of having elaborated a metaphysical speculative discourse on person, he chose to work out a phenomenological presentation. In this way Maritain with his own demonstrative methodology and John Paul II with his own phenomenological methodology can complement each other in offering us a fuller understanding of what person involves.

5. REASON FOR DIFFERENCES IN PERSPECTIVE AND METHOLODOGY

The difference in the crisis of the person when Maritain started to work out his personalism and when John Paul II developed his own personalism explains why Maritain used the *theoria* approach, the object grasped and understood in its being, while John-Paul II concentrated on the *praxis* approach, the action experienced in consciousness and analyzed to bring out the ground of being. It should be kept in mind that both forms of personalism, having their foundation in the philosophy of Thomas Aquinas, emphasized the importance of the person as being in justifying the reality of the person and in assuring the fulfillment of the person. Without an insight into the person as being, philosophy would be reduced to an illusion and the pitfalls of ideosophers, according to Maritain. Without the recognition of the human subject in its ontological reality, in its existence and its acts, philosophy would be reduced to an empty and unfounded enterprise, according to John Paul II. An integral humanist personalism need not take advantage of phenomenology or other modern and contemporary methodologies, according to Maritain, because the very crisis created at the beginning of the twentieth century is the outcome of these methodologies. What was at stake with the *Personalism* of Renouvier and the various conceptions about the human being was that modern and contemporary philosophies denied the human its uniqueness as a being, as a person, as spiritual, as free, as created, as a center in the universe, as open to God and destined for immortality. It became important to rethink the *theoria* enterprise of speculative philosophy to overcome the limitations imposed on the person by modern philosophers. Once having demonstrated the unique nature of the person and its unique value, Maritain could develop a view of the society in which man becomes perfect.

The crisis faced by John Paul II was not so much a questioning of the nature of person as a kind of being, as the preventing of the person from the exercise of the actions which, in the new view of person, were the conditions for the becoming of a person. The alienation of person from itself in the denial of the opportunity to become a person through its acting becomes the crisis to be overcome, instead of the crisis coming from the denial of the objective spiritual nature of person. Just as Maritain took up the challenge of the crisis from the perspective of the nature of person by thinking through person-being within the methodology of a philosophy of being, so also John Paul II took up the challenge of the crisis from the perspective at the acting person by bringing out the exigencies of the person-acting within the methodology of the philosophy of acting. The theoria approach is replaced by the praxis approach. The richness of the phenomenological analysis made by John Paul II brings out an awareness of person which is quite different in its emphasis from the metaphysical notion of person as human subject (even though he often affirms this fact), and which is in a position to be conscious of itself in a way that could bring about a liberation of the self from oppression to overcome the alienation the person is subjected to when the exigency of the self for action is denied. The phenomenological analysis of the person-acting solves the praxis crisis. Since the crisis in the later part of the twentieth century is one of praxis, where the role of action is crucial to the becoming person, John Paul II emphasizes the need of a new starting point that will allow for a new methodology and a new perspective in the study of person. Since the methodology is not speculative and since the perspective is not metaphysical, there is a need to avoid philosophy of nature and cosmology as a starting point in the philosophical reflection and to start instead with anthropology and problems of ethics. In dealing with the person as human subject and as human self, it becomes important to rethink the problems of the human acting with others both as a social being cooperating with others in society towards a common goal and as a communal being participating and communing with others in a community of persons becoming persons. In this sense, the personalism of John Paul ends up having a different perspective than is found in Maritain on the notion of person and a different methodological approach in resolving the problems in the face of the crisis they each confronted. It is good to distinguish their contributions to the Christian philosophy enterprise before uniting their observations to obtain a more comprehensive view of person.

6.   COMPLEMENTARY OF THE CONTRIBUTIONS OF JOHN PAUL II AND MARITAIN TO CHRISTIAN PERSONALISM

When we think of personalism the name Mounier comes to mind. The person understood in both a personalist perspective and a communitarian perspective plays a central role in his approach to life, which is given an existentialist and phenomenological analysis. The influence of Max Scheler is felt in the Mounier Personalism through his disciple Paul Landsberg. Maritain was instrumental in the founding of *Esprit* as advisor and friend to Mounier. Both Mounier and Maritain were influential in the philosophical scene in Poland. John Paul has recognized publicly the importance of Maritain today as an interpreter and developer of the philosophy of Thomas Aquinas in the contemporary world. Both Maritain and John Paul II stress that the value of the philosophy of Thomas Aquinas for the twentieth century is due to its openness to further developments in meeting new challenges. Given the richness of the philosophical developments of Maritain in the context of an objectivist integral humanist personalism, it could be that the elaborations missing in John Paul II concerning what he considers indispensable to his phenomenological synthetic existential personalism, namely, the metaphysical human subject, could be found in Maritain. It could also be that the richness of the philosophical developments of John Paul could serve to open up Maritain's philosophy to new opportunities. With Maritain, John Paul II could take a step back to have the material needed for his foundations and with John Paul II, Maritain could take a step forward to deal with contemporary concerns. John Paul II seeks an adequate, synthetic, and integrated Thomistic personalism where the contributions of the phenomenological analysis keep a solid basis in the foundation of the human subject provided by the philosophy of being. The resulting whole which respects the nature of the creature and which appeals to the consciousness of the acting person overcomes contradiction. As we look at the contributions to personalism of Thomas Aquinas, Maritain, Mounier, Scheler and John Paul II we wonder if another opportunity would not be an *Integral Personalism* which, instead of reducing the phenomenological to the

metaphysical for its authenticity, as in John Paul, or excluding the phenomenological in favor of the metaphysical because of its truth, as in Maritain,
opens up to the possibility of the ambiguity within the whole person resulting
from the overlapping of the metaphysical and of the phenomenological (along
with the phenomenal). The person, then, in its triadic opportunity can be a
sign of self-contradiction in the process of self-appropriation. While developing
Thomistic Personalism beyond the achievements of Maritain and John Paul
II, this integral personalism could face up to the challenge of the present-day
crisis in which philosophizing Christians find themselves as Catholics in the
world today.

7.   BEYOND MARITAIN'S INTEGRAL HUMANISM AND
JOHN PAUL'S INTEGRATED PERSONALISM TO
GENDREAU'S INTEGRAL PERSONALISM

Emmanuel Mounier with his emphasis on the person as conscious, free
and creative in the perspective of the personalist and communitarian context
would suggest the possibility of taking seriously that other pole of our whole
self coexisting within the self with the metaphysical pole of the philosophy
of being. Under the influence of Mounier the contemporary philosopher dealing
with the 1980 crisis arising from the requirements of the philosophy of person-
being and from the exigencies of philosophy of person-acting could be called
upon to develop an integral personalism. The elements of personalist and
communitarian in an existentialist phenomenological context would impose
themselves on our attention. However, Maritain emphasized the person as an
actuality in existence operating as an individual and a person, as a kind of
being which is an individual substance of a rational nature achieving its
perfection by finding fulfillment with the help of other human beings in society
and in community. He would therefore remind us that in spite of the suggestion
from modern philosophy of the importance of the subjective rationalist or empiri-
cist features of the self and in spite of the appeal of contemporary philosophy
concerning the importance of the subjectivity implied in the lived experience
with the consciousness of the self in its thrust of intentionality, the only
philosophizing worthy of the name would be the metaphysical philosophy of
being as the means of developing a philosophy of the person. With Maritain
as an intellectual master one cannot let go of the metaphysically thought-
through philosophy of being, and with Mounier as an intellectual guide one
cannot leave aside the phenomenologically developed philosophy of acting.
But with Wojtyla (John Paul II) a new possibility emerges quite clearly (though
not intended) from the integrated, synthetic, and adequate personalism proposed
as requiring the development of a phenomenological analysis of the person
acting to bring out the self as a conscious agent of consciously exercised
activity, having the conscious awareness of the self as unique agent of his
own activities beyond the still recognized dynamism of the human subject
with its determination in being and its finality in its acts. In spite of his

emphasis on the unity of the two poles of the human subject with its finality and the human self with its consciousness of its own agency in the acting, and in spite of his unequivocal claim that, without the metaphysical philosophy of being, the basic human thrust would fall short of the personal in its realization as consciousness and in its participation in community, Wojtyla leaves us unintentionally (it should be made very clear) with an inkling for a new opportunity. This new opportunity is to consider the two poles of the person-being and the person-acting (keeping in mind the person-phenomenally-appearing) as overlapping instead of reduced or fused into a harmoniously coordinated self, so that instead of a primacy given to being in determining the true, the good, the beautiful as well as the objective reality, the moral doing and the esthetic endeavor, the primacy would be given to the whole person with the risk of the person's becoming a sign of self-contradiction in the living of life in the real world of persons.

While Integral Personalism is not within the intention of John Paul's new personalism, this personalism offers food for thought in that direction by opening new vistas for a personalist philosophy. John Paul's integrated, synthetic, and adequate personalism, in emphasizing the human exigency for a way of being a person that involves a contemporary structuralist phenomenological base through consciousness, establishes the validity and the reality of that pole of personhood, and in emphasizing the human requirement for a way of being a person which involves a classical mediaeval objectivistic base through being, confirms the validity and the reality of that pole of personhood. However, the phenomenological reduction which implies in the philosophy of person-acting the philosophy of being as the ground for the consciously aware, accomplished person, and the objectivistic presupposition of the actuality in reality of a being with its acts tending towards finality as found in a philosophy of being which permeates and determines the truth, value and beauty for the whole person in its personalistic pole and in its objectivistic pole, make clear that this is a closed personalism which is not open to the possibility of a modern subjective base or a contemporary subjectivity base to created meaningfulness in the operating subject which is becoming operational on the basis of principles other than those coming from a philosophy of being and leading to opposite possibilities and opportunities in the living of a fully personalist life. It would seem clear that the commitment to this closed personalism with its base in the Thomistic, whether it be that of the classical objectivist integral humanism of Maritain or the classical-contemporary integrated personalism of John Paul, makes inappropriate, within the context of the philosophy involved, any suggestions of openness to a different base and to alternative opportunities coming out of these other bases considered in themselves as a new perspective, as in a process philosophy, a phenomenological personalist approach, and an existentialist situationist ethics, or as overlapping with the classical mediaeval metaphysical, as in integral personalism. Furthermore, the present-day post-Vatican II doctrinal teachings of the institutional Catholic Church under the guidance of John Paul II would clearly seem to impose the same restrictions. The lived experience of the people of God and the research and findings of the theologians, however, seem to indicate that the tie-in between the metaphysical philosophy of being and the phenomenological philosophy of acting, with the primacy required for the Aristotelian, Stoic, and Thomist objectivist base in the tradition of an intellectualist metaphysical philosophy of person-being, could and perhaps even should be loosened up. Recognizing the importance and the on-going value of the intellectualist objectivist metaphysical philosophy of person-being, alive and greatly enriched since the fourth century within the Catholic tradition, and recognizing the importance of the newly discovered structuralist bases within the context of praxis—in a philosophy of person-acting—for a renewal and intensification of a meaningful personalist life within the Church in the world, Integral Personalism faces up to the new crisis in fundamentals of the last decades of the twentieth century. In the normal course of events there is much value for the becoming person in keeping a steady course on the basis of a Thomism concretely ensconced in the objective reality created by God which man can know as it is and from which man can know what he is to do, and enriched with the phenomenological opportunities made available in the analysis of consciousness. Even then, the change in conceptual possibility in the history of Western culture and the variety of conceptual possibilities in the whole universe, along with the pluralism of the objectivity brought out in the subjectivity of lived human experience, might call for a rethinking of the closed personalism which, however, limits itself to the requirements of the metaphysical being. And since the human being cannot live by truth alone and the good alone as determined by the metaphysical philosophy of being, there is a need, if the metaphysical philosophy of being is still to play a role in our lives and keep the basic respect due it, that an integral personalism be developed which recognizes that especially in borderline cases of sexuality, of social justice, of Christian commitment and mystical experience there is a unique value in being a sign of self-contradiction in developing a total perspective leading to a wholesome life for the whole person. This Integral Personalism seems a way of philosophizing which is responsive to the times.

Saint Thomas and the Principle of Causality

LAWRENCE DEWAN, O.P.
Collège dominicain de philosophie et
de théologie d'Ottawa

Il y a déjà eu quelques débats relatifs à l'existence du principe de causalité *et au rôle qu'un tel principe pourrait jouer dans une métaphysique thomiste. Dans la même veine, l'auteur présente d'abord la conception qu'avait saint Thomas du rôle et de la responsabilité de la métaphysique en ce qui concerne la discussion et la défense des premiers principes de la connaissance démonstrative; et il note aussi l'espèce de proposition qui, selon lui, constitue un tel principe.*

De là, il examine le principe un effet dépend de sa cause, *parce que saint Thomas lui-même se servait de ce principe de façon non négligeable et qu'il a pris la peine de nous en laisser une réflexion brève mais pénétrante, où il en expose les multiples sens et les degrés d'intelligibilité. Enfin il s'interroge à savoir si ce principe pourrait contribuer à résoudre la controverse sur la causalité au sein de la philosophie moderne, controverse suscitée surtout par Hume. Et la réponse est affirmative. À cet effet, il introduit certaines considérations de saint Thomas à propos des divers modes d'être de l'objet de l'intelligence humaine.*

INTRODUCTION

Jacques Maritain, looking back over half a century of philosophizing by Thomists, singled out as particularly remarkable Étienne Gilson's *Esprit de la philosophie médiévale* and Fr. Réginald Garrigou-Lagrange's *La philosophie de l'être et le sens commun.*[1] His interest in this latter work is not surprising when one considers his own *Sept leçons sur l'être et les premiers principes de la raison spéculative.*[2] Both books exhibit a fervent interest in and defense of the principles of identity, sufficient reason, finality, and causality.[3]

On the other hand, Étienne Gilson did not show this sort of interest in such principles. Rather, especially in "Les principes et les causes," he argued that such an interest is somewhat foreign to the type of metaphysics one finds in the writings of St. Thomas. It is not that St. Thomas would deny any of the propositions presented as first principles of speculative reason by these Thomists. It is rather that the modern interest in these propositions is symptomatic of a certain tendency to look at knowing as having some sort of independence vis-à-vis being itself. Gilson saw it as important to call attention back from the consideration of such seeming axioms to the root of all metaphysical discussion, namely, being itself.[4] In the wake of Gilson's paper, Joseph Owens

---

1. See Jacques Maritain, *Le paysan de la Garonne*, Paris, Desclée de Brouwer, 1966, p. 201, n. 1. The work of Fr. Garrigou-Lagrange is actually entitled *Le sens commun, la philosophie de l'être et les formules dogmatiques*, Paris, Desclée de Brouwer, 1909.
2. Jacques Maritain, *Sept leçons sur l'être et les premiers principes de la raison spéculative*, Paris, Téqui, 1932-1933.
3. For earlier references to Garrigou-Lagrange's book, see Maritain's *La philosophie bergsonienne* (4th ed.), Paris, Téqui, 1948, p. 130, n. 1. This work dates from 1913, and the references to Garrigou-Lagrange are very probably original; see also Maritain's essay "La vie propre de l'intelligence et l'erreur idéaliste" (dated 1924), in *Réflexions sur l'intelligence et sur sa vie propre* (2nd ed.), Paris, Nouvelle librairie nationale, 1926, p. 71, n. 1 (and see pp. 69-77, as regards the subject of the present essay).
4. Étienne Gilson, "Les principes et les causes," *Revue thomiste* 52 (1952), pp. 39-63: "...tout dépend du type de métaphysique auquel l'intellect donne son assentiment et il se peut fort bien que le principe de causalité soit utilement explicité dans l'une alors qu'une autre n'éprouvera pas le besoin de le formuler à part. Généralement parlant, ce principe semblera d'autant plus utile qu'une métaphysique mettra l'accent sur la nécessité formelle des preuves plutôt que sur la nécessité réelle qu'impose à l'intellect la nature même de l'actuellement existant." (p. 61)

published his "The Causal Proposition—Principle or Conclusion?" in which he maintained that the causal proposition, that is, some such proposition as "everything whose existence is other than its essence has its existence from something else," actually is presented by St. Thomas as the conclusion of a strict demonstration.[5] Referring expressly to Maritain's contention that the proposition "everything contingent must be caused" is a first principle of speculative reason, Fr. Owens argued that it required a demonstration.[6]

In the present paper, I propose to assemble some materials from the writings of St. Thomas which may help us form a more definite conception of the procedure in metaphysics. What kind of discussion of principles of knowledge might the metaphysician be expected to provide? Among these principles, what would count as a "principle of causality"? Such an enterprise cannot be amiss when one considers how influential the Humean view has been (i.e., that cause and effect are impossible as objects of knowledge).[7]

1. THE ARISTOTELIAN *APORIA* AND ITS SOLUTION

Commenting on Aristotle's *Metaphysics*, book 5, St. Thomas notes the secondary meaning of the word "principle" as applying to what comes first in the order of our knowing:

> But in resemblance to the order which is considered in exterior motions, there is also remarked a certain order in the knowing of things; and especially according as our intellect has some likeness of motion, proceeding discursively from principles to conclusions. *And therefore "principles" is said in another way: "that whence first a thing is known"*; thus, we call "principles" *of demonstration the suppositions*, i.e. the axioms and postulates.[8]

---

5. Joseph Owens C. Ss. R., "The Causal Proposition—Principle or Conclusion?", *The Modern Schoolman* 32 (1955), pp. 159-171, 257-270, 323-339; cf. the same author's "The Causal Proposition Revisited," *The Modern Schoolman* 44 (1966-67), pp. 143-151.

6. See Owens, "The Causal Proposition—Principle or Conclusion?", p. 336, n. 95. Concerning the history of the controversies among Thomists in recent times as regards the principle of causality, see Raymond Laverdière, *Le principe de causalité. Recherches thomistes récentes*, Paris, Vrin (Bibliothèque thomiste, 39), 1969.

7. See David Hume, *An Enquiry concerning Human Understanding*, Sect. VII, Part II (in ed. L. A. Selby-Bigge, Oxford [2nd ed.], Clarendon Press, 1902): "We have sought in vain for an idea of power or necessary connexion in all the sources from which we could suppose it to be derived. . . . So that, upon the whole, there appears not, throughout all nature, any one instance of connexion which is conceivable by us. All events seem entirely loose and separate. One event follows another; but we never can observe any tie between them . . . " (para. 58, pp. 73-74). He goes on, of course, to locate the source of our idea in the mind's experience of its own habitual anticipations: "This connexion, therefore, which we *feel* in the mind, this customary transition of the imagination from one object to its usual attendant, is the sentiment or impression from which we form the idea of power or necessary connection." (para. 59, p. 75).

8. See St. Thomas Aquinas, *In Metaphysicam Aristotelis commentarium* 5.1.759, concerning Aristotle, *Metaph.* 5.1 (1013a14-16). This work of St. Thomas will henceforth be cited as "CM"; the third number in the references is to the paragraph in the edition of M.-R. Cathala, O.P., Turin (3rd ed.), Marietti, 1935. Italics in our quotation indicate the words of Aristotle being explained.

However, it is in connection with the discussions of difficulties and questions in Aristotle's book 3 that we see most reflection by St. Thomas on the metaphysician's interest in such principles. Aristotle, compiling the questions in his first chapter, asks in second place: supposing that this science is to consider the "first principles," as was said in book 1; does that mean it is to consider only the first principles of substance, or does it also pertain to this science to consider the "first principles of demonstration," for example, that this science would consider whether it comes about that one and the same thing be simultaneously affirmed and denied, or not; and similarly with the other first and self-evident principles of demonstration? [*de aliis demonstrationis principiis primis et per se notis*][9] St. Thomas here follows Aristotle in speaking of a multiplicity of such first principles, though he gives no indication for the moment as to what he thinks the others are.

A little later, when Aristotle spells out the problem, by pointing out arguments on both sides, St. Thomas notes that Aristotle first tells us what he means by the principles of demonstration:

> And he says that they are *the common* conceptions of all, *from which proceed all demonstrations*, inasmuch as (i.e.) the particular principles of the proper demonstrated conclusions have solidity in virtue of the common principles.[10]

Here, St. Thomas has replaced Aristotle's expression "common opinions" with "common conceptions," a vocabulary coming from Boethius' *De hebdomadibus*.[11] This association will be developed further later on.

Aristotle gives us here a further example of such a principle, viz. "it is impossible for the same thing at once to be and not to be," and St. Thomas describes it as "another principle."[12]

We should also note that at the end of his presentation here, St. Thomas sketches what will be Aristotle's answer in book 4, saying that, yes, it does belong to the philosopher to consider the axioms, inasmuch as it belongs to him to consider being in general [*ens in communi*], to which such first principles properly [*per se*] pertain. This relation to *ens* is most apparent [*maxime apparet*] in the case of the "most first principle" [*maxime primum principium*], viz. that it is impossible for the same to be and not to be.[13] This last remark

---

9. See CM 3.2.347, concerning Aristotle, *Metaph.* 3.1 (995b6-10).
10. CM 3.5.387, concerning Aristotle, *Metaph.* 3.2 (996b28) (italics indicate words of Aristotle).
11. See St. Thomas Aquinas, *In librum Boetii De hebdomadibus expositio, lect.* 1 (in ed. M. Calcaterra, O.P., *Opuscula Theologica*, vol. II, Turin/Rome, Marietti, 1954, nos. 14-18.
12. CM 3.5.387 concerning Aristotle, *Metaph.* 3.2 (996b29-31): "Et exemplificat de primis principiis maxime sicut quod necesse est de unoquoque aut affirmare aut negare. Et aliud principium est quod impossibile est idem simul esse et non esse."
13. CM 3.5392: "Hanc autem quaestionem determinat Philosophus in quarto huius; et dicit, quod ad philosophum potius pertinet consideratio dignitatum, inquantum ad ipsum pertinet consideratio entis in communi, ad quod per se pertinent huiusmodi principia prima, ut maxime apparet in eo quod est maxime primum principium, scilicet quod impossibile est idem esse et non esse. . . ."

is important as indicating that one principle is more obviously related to *ens* than another, even though both are first principles of demonstration.

If we turn now to St. Thomas's book 4, *lectio* 5, we find not only a presentation of Aristotle's doctrine that it is for metaphysics to consider generally *all* the principles of demonstration (and not merely the absolutely first), but also, and more important, a digression by St. Thomas so as to make clear the doctrine at issue. We should notice that Aristotle himself relates the type of propositions he has in mind to the practice of the mathematicians. He says he is speaking about what in mathematics are called "axioms." The relation to mathematics is made, St. Thomas tells us, because mathematical sciences have more certain demonstrations, and make a more obvious use of such *per se nota* propositions, reducing all their demonstrations to such principles.[14]

St. Thomas's digression is intended to clarify the link between the science that treats of substance as such and the science that treats of the first principles of demonstration. In order to do so, he primarily considers what constitutes a first principle of demonstration, i.e., that it is known *to all*, because it is about the most common things. And this is then related to metaphysics as treating of the common terms.

Thus, he begins by telling us that those propositions are known by virtue of themselves [*per se notae*] which are immediately known, upon the terms out of which they are composed being known (and for this he refers us to *Posterior Analytics*, book 1).[15] This immediate knowing happens in the case of those propositions in which the predicate is included in the definition of the subject, or in which the predicate is the same as the subject.[16] St. Thomas then points out that it happens that a proposition be *per se nota* in itself but not to all. Some people may be in ignorance of the definition of the predicate and of the subject. (And here he cites Boethius' *De hebdomadibus*, as to the existence of propositions *per se notae* only to the wise.) Those propositions are *per se notae* to all whose terms fall into the conception of all [*in conceptionem omnium cadunt*], i.e., which occur to the mind of anyone who thinks (it seems to me that St. Thomas means by "all" all minds rather than all things, in view of the reason he goes on to give). These terms are *the common ones*

---

14.   CM 4.5.588, concerning Aristotle, *Metaph.* 4.3 (1005a19-21): "Appropriat autem ista principia magis mathematicis scientiis, quia certiores demonstrationes habent, et manifestius istis principiis per se notis utuntur, omnes suas demonstrationes ad haec principia resolventes."

15.   See St. Thomas Aquinas, *In Aristotelis libros Posteriorum analyticorum expositio* 1.7.67 [8], concerning Aristotle, 1.3 (72b24) (the third number in the reference to St. Thomas is to the paragraph in ed. R.M. Spiazzi, O.P., Rome/Turin, Marietti 1955 (Leonine manual); cf. ibid., 1.5.50 [7], concerning Aristotle at 1.2 (72a15-19).

16.   We might underline how constant St. Thomas is concerning this feature of first principles of demonstration. They are in the *first* mode of *per se* predication: see *In Post. an.* 1.10.84 [3], concerning Aristotle, 1.4 (73a34-37). Still, it should also be noticed that in any demonstration one of the premises must be in the *fourth* mode of *per se* predication (the predicate expressing some sort of *cause* of the subject): see *In Post. an.* 1.13.111 [3].

[*communia*], since our knowledge proceeds from common things to proper things (for this, he refers us to *Physics*, book 1).[17] Thus, those porportions are first principles of demonstration which are composed of common terms. Such terms are "whole" and "part" which yield the principle: "a whole is greater than its parts"; and "equal" and "unequal," yielding: "what are equal to one and the same thing are equal to each other." And the same idea holds for similar cases. It is because the philosopher, i.e., the metaphysician, is the one to whom it belongs to consider such common terms that it belongs to him to consider these principles.

St. Thomas concludes the digression by pointing out the type of handling such propositions receive from the metaphysician. He does not demonstrate them, but rather treats of the notions of their terms, saying what is a whole and what is a part. St. Thomas does not say anything about why such treatment is required.[18]

From all of this, then, we see the metaphysician as treating of a multiplicity of such principles, composed of common terms, and having the predicate included in the definition of the subject. Exploration of St. Thomas's other writings only serves to confirm and somewhat expand this doctrine. Thus, some texts stress the order to be found among the multiplicity of such first

---

17. See St. Thomas Aquinas, *In octo libros Physicorum Aristotelis expositio* (ed. P.M. Maggiòlo, O.P., Turin/Rome, Marietti, 1954; Leonine manual) 1.1.6-8 For my use of the word "thing," in the expression "common things," see St. Thomas, *In Post. an.* 1.20.171 [5]: "Philosophia enim prima est de communibus, quia eius consideratio est circa ipsas res communes, scilicet circa ens et partes et passiones entis."

18. CM 4.5.595: ". . . philosophi erit considerare de omni substantia inquantum huiusmodi, et de primis syllogismorum principiis. Ad huius autem evidentiam sciendum, quod propositiones per se notae sunt, quae statim notis terminis cognoscuntur, ut dicitur primo Posteriorum. Hoc autem contingit in illis propositionibus in quibus praedicatum ponitur in definitione subiecti, vel praedicatum est idem subiecto.—Sed contingit aliquam propositionem quantum in se est esse per se notam, non tamen esse per se notam omnibus, qui ignorant definitionem praedicati et subiecti. Unde Boetius dicit in libro de Hebdomadibus, quod quaedam sunt per se nota sapientibus quae non sunt per se nota omnibus. Illa autem sunt per se nota omnibus, quorum termini in conceptionem omnium cadunt. Huiusmodi autem sunt communia, eo quod nostra cognitio a communibus ad propria pervenit, ut dicitur in primo Physicorum. Et ideo istae propositiones sunt prima demonstrationum principia, quae componuntur ex terminis communibus, sicut totum et pars, ut Omne totum est maius sua parte; et sicut aequale et inaequale, ut Quae uni et eidem sunt aequalia, sibi sunt aequalia. Et eadem ratio est de similibus. Et quia huiusmodi communes termini pertinent ad considerationem philosophi, ideo haec principia de consideratione philosophi sunt.—Determinat autem ea philosophus non demonstrando, sed rationes terminorum tradendo, ut quid totum et quid pars et sic de aliis. Hoc autem cognito, veritas praedictorum principiorum manifesta relinquitur." On this last point, cf. CM 3.5.392: ". . . philosophus non considerat huiusmodi principia tamquam faciens ea scire definiendo vel absolute demonstrando; sed solum elenchice, idest contradicendo disputative negantibus ea, ut in quarto dicetur."

For a modern example of a defense of "a whole is greater than its parts," see Charles De Koninck, "Random Reflections on Science and Calculation," *Laval théologique et philosophique* 12 (1956), pp. 96-100 (against Bertrand Russell).

See also CM 11.4.2208 and 2210: the study of quantity as quantity is proper to the metaphysician.

principles, an order which corresponds to the order of objects in human intellectual apprehension.[19]

2.   THE PRINCIPLE OF CAUSALITY

I propose for discussion, not as the only causal principle, but certainly as a causal principle, the proposition: "an effect depends on its cause." This is not a principle simply invented in imitation of "a whole is greater than its part," for the purposes of the present reflections. We find St. Thomas using it at important moments. Thus, in *Summa theologiae* 1.2.2, when explaining the possibility of demonstrating the existence of God, he makes it the basic of the argument. We read:

> . . . from any effect it can be demonstrated that its proper cause exists, if, that is, the effects of that [cause] are better known to us; because, since *effects depend on the cause*, if the effect is posited, the cause must exist by priority [*praeexistere*].[20]

This consideration thus commands the entire discussion of the five ways.

Elsewhere in the same work, speaking of the need for every creature to be conserved in its being by God, he once more makes our proposition the principle of the argument:

> . . . the being [*esse*] of every creature depends on God . . . For *every effect depends on its cause, according as it is its cause.* . . .[21]

Still, concerning the proposition itself there is no discussion in these passages. It is simply used as a principle, and in fact is understood within the confines of efficient causality, not as applying to all the types of causal relation.

Fortunately, on at least one occasion, St. Thomas provides us with a brief study of the proposition. This is in the slightly earlier *De potentia* presentation of God's conservation of creatures. Here is the passage which interests us:

> . . . For it is necessary that *an effect depend on its cause*. For this belongs to the notion of effect and cause;[22] which manifestly appears in formal and material causes. For, any

---

19.   See especially St. Thomas Aquinas, *Summa theologiae* (henceforth ST), 1-2.94.2 (ed. Ottawa, Commissio Piana, 1953): "In his autem quae in apprehensione hominum cadunt, quidam ordo invenitur. Nam illud quod primo cadit in apprehensione est ens. . . " (1225b6-9).

20.   ST 1.2.2: "Ex quolibet autem effectu potest demonstrari propriam causam eius esse, si tamen eius effectus sint magis noti quoad nos; quia, cum *effectus dependeant a causa*, posito effectu necesse est causam praeexistere" (our italics).

21.   ST 1.104.1 (ed. Ottawa, 622b36-38): "Omnis enim effectus dependet a sua causa secundum quod est causa eius."

22.   See also St. Thomas, *In Phys.* 1.1.5 [5]: ". . . causae autem dicuntur ex quibus aliqua dependent secundum suum esse vel fieri. . . " In this text, St. Thomas is aiming to say what precisely is said by the word "cause" as distinct from "element" and "principle." He goes on to say that Aristotle seems to be using "element" for the material cause, "principle" for the efficient cause, and "cause" for the formal and final cause: the reason? "per *causas* autem videtur intelligere causas formales et finales, a quibus maxime dependent res secundum suum esse et fieri. . . " (ibid.) He is commenting on Aristotle at *Phys.* 1.1 (184a11-12).

material or formal principle being subtracted, the thing immediately ceases to be, because such principles enter into the essence of the thing.—But it is necessary that there be the same judgment concerning efficient causes as concerning formal or material [causes]. For the efficient cause is cause of the thing according as it induces the form or disposes the matter. Hence, there is the same dependence of the thing with respect to the efficient cause as there is with respect to the matter and the form, since it is through one of them [i.e. the matter or the from] that it [i.e. the thing] depends on the other [i.e. the efficient cause].—But it is necessary that there be the same judgment concerning final causes as concerning the efficient cause: for the end is a cause only inasmuch as it moves the efficient cause to act: for it is not first in being [esse], but only in intention. Hence, where there is no action, there is no final cause. . . . [23]

What is of interest here especially is the *gradual* presentation of "an effect depends on its cause." We have, it would seem, three different levels of judgment in the matter. It *appears manifestly (manifeste apparet)*[24] as regards the formal and material causes. If we take away either of them, the thing no longer has being. The reason for this is that matter and form are parts of the essence, enter into the essence. The essence, as St. Thomas said in the *De ente*, is that in which and through which a being *(ens)* has being *(esse)*.[25] We see how directly we have to do here with what we mean by "a being *(ens)*." As St. Thomas says elsewhere, "something is called 'caused'

---

23.   St. Thomas, *De potentia* 5.1: "Effectum enim a sua causa dependere oportet. Hoc enim est de ratione effectus et causae: quod quidem in causis formalibus et materialibus manifeste apparet. Quocumque enim materiali vel formali principio subtracto, res statim esse desinit, cum huiusmodi principia intrent essentiam rei.—Idem autem iudicium oportet esse de causis efficientibus, et formalibus vel materialibus. Nam efficiens est causa rei secundum quod formam inducit, vel materiam disponit. Unde eadem dependentia rei est ad efficiens, et ad materiam et formam, cum per unum eorum ab altero dependeat. De finalibus autem causis oportet etiam idem esse iudicium quod de causa efficiente. Nam finis non est causa, nisi secundum quod movet efficientem ad agendum; non enim est primum in esse, sed in intentione solum. Unde et ubi non est actio, non est causa finalis, ut patet in III *Metaph.*"

24.   Joseph Owens, in "The Causal Proposition—Principle or Conclusion?", p. 160, n. 1, after speaking of the controversy concerning the causal proposition as having its beginning in Hume's separating two components of the Lockean idea of effect, namely "beginning to exist" and "operation of some other being," goes on: "This background restricts the controversy to efficient causality, and rightly so. The causality of the intrinsic causes, material and formal, is self-evident once these components of a thing are distinctly grasped, while the final cause and the exemplar cause exercise their causality through the efficient cause. The difficulty lies in showing how a thing necessarily contains a relation to an efficient cause which produced it, even though that efficient causality, except in the cases of one's own conscious activity, is not immediately evident." On the one hand, Fr. Owens' difficulty is not the one presented by Hume, since Fr. Owens thinks he has immediate evidence of the efficient causality which he exercises in his own conscious activity. On the other hand, his position is very different from that of St. Thomas, for whom the efficient causality of sensible bodies is evident: ". . . sensibiliter apparet aliqua corpora esse activa . . ." (ST 1.115.1) But above all it seems to me wrong to cut off the discussion from formal causality. The *De potentia* text shows this. Charles De Koninck, *The Hollow Universe*. London, Oxford University Press, 1960, p. 100, n. 1, appreciates the necessity of beginning any critical discussion of causality with the material and formal causes.

25.   St. Thomas Aquinas, *De ente et essentia*, c. 1, lines 50-52 (*Opera omnia*, t. 43, Rome, Editori di San Tommaso, 1976): "Sed essentia dicitur secundum quod per eam et in ea ens habet esse."

because it has a cause of its being (*esse*)"[26] and "a cause is that upon which the *esse* of something else follows."[27]

"Effect" here is the thing, and "cause" means the thing's own form, or the thing's own matter.[28] To say that an effect depends on its cause is first of all to say that the being of a thing depends[29] on its form.[30]

This dependence is so immediate that, if there is a problem here, it is to see it as dependence at all. We see the need for the form in such a strong way that we scarcely see any duality. That is, from the point of view of the primacy of sense cognition for human beings, we are better off where causes are sensibly diverse things. We are better off the more "extrinsic" the cause is. Thus, in *Metaphysics* 7.17, Aristotle argues that the form is cause of being, because to say what a thing is, is really to say "why is the wood a house," where the answer might be "because of the activity of the builder" or "for the sheltering of a family." That is, he assimilates formal causality to efficient or final causality, where the duality of cause and effect is more evident.[31] But St. Thomas is here speaking from the viewpoint of intellect as first of all grasping the quiddity of a thing.[32] The first intelligible conception of what

---

26. St. Thomas Aquinas, *In Post. an.* 2.7.471 [2], concerning Aristotle, 2.8 (93a4-7): ". . . propter hoc enim dicitur aliquid causatum, quod habet causam sui esse. Haec autem causa essendi aut est eadem, scilicet cum essentia ipsius rei, aut alia. Eadem quidem, sicut forma et materia, quae sunt partes essentiae; alia vero, sicut efficiens et finis; quae duae causae sunt quodammodo causae formae et materiae, nam agens operatur propter finem et unit formam materiae."

27. St. Thomas Aquinas, *In Phys.* 2.10.240 [15]: ". . . cum causa sit ad quam sequitur esse alterius. . . ." It should not, of course, be thought that it is the *esse* which is the caused thing: it is the subsisting thing, the composite, the thing that has *esse*, which is caused: cf. ST 1.45.4c. and *ad* 1; ST. 1.3.7 *ad* 1.

28. From the properly metaphysical viewpoint, matter is quite secondary: see our paper, "St. Thomas Aquinas against Metaphysical Materialism,"in *Atti del'VIII Congresso Tomistico internazionale. V—Problemi Metafisici* (Studi Tomisticci 14), Città del Vaticano, 1982: Libreria Editrice Vaticana, especially pp. 428-434. Nevertheless, in the order of human learning it is quite important. Cf. De Koninck, *The Hollow Universe*, p. 100, n. 1: ". . . once we have defined cause as 'that upon which something depends in being or becoming', the notion of the material cause is the most obvious and certain, such as the wood of a wooden table; then that of form, e.g. the shape of the table; and any critical discussion of causality should begin with these."

29. Even the word "depends" supposes *understood* the cause/effect situation of the beings we know. One can see this in St. Thomas's CM 5.13, where he is commenting upon Aristotle's presentation of the notions of priority and posteriority. Thus, in para. 950, the first way in which something is prior to another "in being" (*in essendo*) involves the notion of dependence ("*ratione . . . dependentiae*"): "those are called 'prior' which can *be* without others and those [others] cannot be without them"; and in para. 953, all modes of priority and posteriority are said to be reducible to this one. The reason for this reducibility: "For it is clear that the prior do not *depend* on the posterior, the way the converse [is true]. Hence, all prior [things] can in some way be without the posterior [things] and not conversely."

30. See ST 1.75.6 (445b2-6); 1.50.5 (321a8-14).

31. See Aristotle, *Metaph.* 7.17 (1041a25-b9). It seems to me the reduction of form to agent and end is important in this passage, even though in another way, "logically," it is the agent and end which are assimilated to the form ("what the thing is").

32. See ST 1.85.8 (534b5-14); 1.85.6 (532b39-42); 1.85.5 (531b12-19).

is in fact causal dependence is the dependence of a thing on its matter and on its form (on its form primarily). That is, just as the first conception of all is *ens*, so the first conception of a cause is of form: "... 'a being' conveys no causal stance except that of the formal cause. ... "[33] Notice that we are here considering the order of being, not the order expressed most properly by the word "cause." We know that, according to St. Thomas, it is the final cause which is first in the order of causality as such: the final cause is the cause of the causality of all the other causes, and the good is prior to being in the order of causality.[34]

"An effect depends on its cause" thus is first of all expressive of the unity of a being composed out of matter and form. The proposition expresses a *per se* unity, that of a substance itself. Still, it does more than that. It expresses dependence and priority. It means that if one were to take away the form or the matter, one would no longer have that thing. The being of the thing, the *esse* of the thing is being considered, and is being seen as following from the matter and the form.[35]

We could say that the proposition "an effect depends on its cause," taken as referring to the composite of matter and form as having its being by virtue of the form, envelops the entire domain of discussion of Aristotle's *Metaphysics* 7: i.e., is it a *"per se"* proposition? Is the essence altogether identical with the thing whose essence it is? In things composed out of matter and form, one has neither pure logical identity nor a mere *"per accidens"*

---

33. See ST 1.5.2 ad 2: "Ens autem non important habitudinem causae nisi formalis tantum, vel inhaerentis vel exemplaris; cuius causalitas non se extendit nisi ad ea quae sunt in actu."
34. See ST 1.5.2 ad 1: "Bonum autem, cum habeat rationem appetibilis, importat habitudinem causae finalis, cuius causalitas prima est, quia agens non agit nisi propter finem, et ab agente materia movetur ad formam; unde dicitur quod finis est causa causarum. Et sic in causando bonum est prius quam ens, sicut finis quam forma . . ." I do not believe that St. Thomas proceeds in the order he does in *De potentia* 5.1 merely because of intelligibility *for us* (as one might think from what De Koninck says, as quoted above, n. 28). Metaphysics, at least as far as it is the knowledge of being (as distinguished from its being knowledge of the first or highest substances: see CM 3.4.384), belongs to the domain wherein intelligibility for us and absolute intelligibility coincide: see St. Thomas, *Sententia libri Ethicorum* (*Opera omnia*, t. 47/2, Rome, 1969: Ad Sanctae Sabinae), 6.5, lines 97-106, concerning Aristotle at 114a16-17: ". . . illa quae est sapientia simpliciter est certissima inter omnes scientias, in quantum scilicet attingit ad prima principia entium, quae secundum se sunt notissima, quamvis aliqua eorum, scilicet immaterialia, sint minus nota quoad nos; universalissima autem principia sunt etiam quoad nos magis nota, sicut ea quae pertinent ad ens in quantum est ens, qorum cognitio pertinet ad sapientiam simpliciter dictam, ut patet in IV Metaphysicae." The causality of form is a more intelligible object, absolutely, than the causality of agent or end. The reason is that the viewpoint of being is absolutely prior to that of cause. See, for this line of thinking, ST 1,82.3 *ad* 1 (503b19-24); 1.13.11 *ad* 2; 1.13.11c. (89a31-b4); 1.16.4 (116b43-49); 1-2.66.3; 2-2.174.2 *ad* 3 (2282b6-9). Just as the word and the notion "virtue" is more properly applied to moral virtue, and yet intellectual virtue is a more noble and intelligible reality, so I would suggest that the formal cause is less properly called "a cause" than the final, but is a more noble and intelligible item than the efficient or final cause as such.
35. See CM 4.2.558; also 9.11.1903.

unity.[36] *In a way*, the form is related to the matter *per accidens*,[37] though in another way they are *per se* one and "a being."[38]

We should remember that the being (*esse*) which the composite has by virtue of the form is neither a *per accidens* accident nor a property (a *per se* accident). It belongs to the domain of substance; it is the act of the essence.[39] Thus, the triad of matter, form, and *esse*[40] included in the signification of "an effect depends on its cause" (within the limits which we are presently giving it) does not break down the *per se* unity. Still, we are expanding the domain of substance so as to consider the really existing substance, the concrete individual or supposit.[41] In this line of thinking one could go so far as to say that "an effect depends on its cause" is nothing less than a realistic principle of identity (substantial unity).[42]

---

36. See CM 7.11.1535-1536; also ST 3.2.6 *ad* 3; *Quodl*.2.2.2 *ad* 1.

37. See CM 7.2.1290, concerning Aristotle at 1029a25: "Sicut enim formae sunt praeter essentiam materiae, et ita quodammodo se habent ad ipsam per accidens, ita negationes formarum. . . ."

38. See CM 8.5.1767, concerning Aristotle at 1045b16-23: "Unde simile est quaerere quae est causa alicuius rei, et quae est causa quod illa res sit una; quia unumquodque inquantum est, unum est, et potentia et actus quodammodo unum sunt. Quod enim est in potentia et actus quodammodo unum sunt. Quod enim est in potentia, fit in actu. Et sic non oportet ea uniri per aliquod vinculum, sicut ea quae sunt penitus diversa. Unde nulla causa est faciens unum ea quae sunt composita ex materia et forma, nisi quod movet potentiam in actum. . . ." See also St. Thomas, *In Aristotelis librum De anima commentarium* 2.1 (para. 234 in ed. A. M. Pirotta, O.P., Turin, Marietti, 1936): "Ostensum est enim in octavo Metaphysicae quod forma per se unitur materiae, sicut actus eius; et idem est materiam uniri formae, quod materiam esse in actu. Et hoc est etiam quod hic dicit, quod cum unum et ens multipliciter dicatur, scilicet de ente in potentia, et de ente in actu, id quod proprie est ens et unum est actus. Nam sicut ens in potentia non est ens simpliciter, sed secundum quid, ita non est unum simpliciter sed secundum quid: sic enim dicitur aliquid unum sicut et ens. Et ideo sicut corpus habet esse per formam, ita et unitur animae immediate, inquantum anima est forma corporis" (concerning Aristotle at 412b6-9)

39. See St. Thomas Aquinas, *De potentia* 5.4 *ad* 3; and especially *Quodl.* 12.5.1: "Sciendum ergo, quod unumquodque quod est in potentia et in actu, fit actu per hoc quod participat actum superiorem. Per hoc autem aliquid maxime fit actu quod participat per similitudinem primum et purum actum. Primus autem actus est esse subsistens per se; unde completionem unumquodque recipit per hoc quod participat esse; unde esse est complementum omnis formae, quia per hoc completur quod habet esse, et habet esse cum est actu: et sic nulla forma est nisi per esse.—Et sic dico quod esse substantiale rei non est accidens, sed actualitas cuiuslibet formae existentis, sive sine materia sive cum materia. . . ."

40. See St. Thomas Aquinas, *Quaestiones de anima*, q. 6 (ed. J. H. Robb, Toronto, Pontifical Institute of Mediaeval Studies, 1968, pp. 111-112): "In substantiis enim ex materia et forma compositis tria invenimus, scilicet materiam, et formam, et tertium esse, cujus quidem principium est forma. Nam materia ex hoc quod recipit formam participat esse. Sic igitur esse consequitur ipsam formam, nec tamen forma est suum esse cum sit ejus principium. Et licet materia non pertingat ad esse nisi per formam, forma tamen, in quantum est forma, non indiget materia ad suum esse cum ipsam formam consequatur esse; sed indiget materia cum sit talis forma quae per se non subsistit."

41. See texts referred to in n. 36.

42. See CM 4.2.561: "Sicut enim partes entis sunt substantia, quantitas, et qualitas, etc., ita et partes unius sunt idem, aequale, et simile. Idem enim unum in substantia est. Aequale, unum

Let us pass on to the second level of judgment, that concerning efficient causes. It is necessary that the judgment be the same concerning them, as concerning material and formal causes. What is interesting here is the *derivation*. We are dealing with the proposition "an effect depends on its cause." One might think that with something so obvious no commentary is needed. On the contrary, we are asked to consider the nature of efficient causality itself. "The efficient cause is a cause according as it induces the form or disposes the matter." Our vision of the *efficiens* as a cause is seen to derive from our vision of matter and form as causes. Only inasmuch as something comes to be associated with the originally seen dependence for being does it get the status of a cause. It is only through dependence on form that the thing has dependence on the efficient cause.

Clearly, St. Thomas sees a *problem* as regards the efficient cause, a problem which (a) does not exist for the material and formal causes, and which (b) the latter can help to resolve. This problem can only be a *seeming dissociability* of effect from cause, a seeming non-dependence of effect on cause, a possibility for the mind to lose sight of the causal relation. This seeming dissociability can have its source only in the key difference between the efficient cause and the material and formal causes, viz. that cause and effect for efficient causality are substantially diverse.[43] The remedy is to focus on the *notion* of efficient cause as that which induces the form. It is only insofar as one grasps a thing *as source of form for another thing* that one grasps it *as* efficient cause. And this is actually to see *the depending of the thing on its form* "stretched out," as it were, beyond the confines of the thing, to another thing.

What this means is that efficient causality is a different grade of intelligible object than is formal causality. Efficient causality is a relation between substances, and a real relation. That is, it has the ontological status of an accident, not a substance. As such, it requires for its intelligibility the presence, in its notion, of things outside its own "essence."[44] It must be presented with the *proper subject* to which it belongs, and the proper term of the relation.[45] The proper subject of efficient causal dependence is the dependent being as a dependent being, and this is seen in the vision of the substantial composite, with its essential causes, the matter and the form. The term of the relation is the other thing *as source of the form* of the dependent being. The proposition

---

in quantitate. Simile, unum in qualitate. Et secundum alias partes entis possent sumi aliae partes unius, si essent nomina posita."

43.   I leave aside the secondary case where the substance is productive of its own accident (i.e., property); see ST 1.77.6.

44.   See St. Thomas Aquinas, CM 7.4, in its entirety, concerning Aristotle, 1030a17-1031a14; see especially CM paras. 1340 and 1352.

45.   See ST. 3.2.7 *ad* 2: ". . . ratio relationis, sicut et motus, dependet ex fine vel termino, sed esse eius dependet a subiecto." Cf. also ST 1.28.2 and *De potentia*, 8.2.

"an effect depends on its cause," understood as expressing the relationship of the effect of the efficient cause to the agent, signifies this vision.

In this way, the proposition has the kind of *per se* character it can have, considering that the quiddity on which it is based is an accident, not a substance. The subject is "an effect," meaning the effect of an efficient cause. Such a term signifies a relation in a subject, i.e., it says "a thing depending on another"; and the predicate merely predicates the definition "depends on another." An effect depends on its cause. One might try saying: "one being depends on another, and then the former is called 'an effect' and the latter 'its cause.'" However, this formulation would seem to *leave out* the proper character of the effect, as a composite of matter and form. Composition out of matter and form[46] is included in the notion of the effect. Thus, the efficient causal meaning of the principle is not *dissociable* from the formal causal meaning. The two meanings do not exist side by side, each independent of the other. One can only *add* the efficient causal meaning to the formal causal meaning. One can only *extend* the originally seen dependence of the thing from inner cause to outer cause.

3.   THE PROBLEM OF HUME

The responsibility of the metaphysician for discussing the causal principle becomes indubitable when the principle is attacked. The most famous such attack in modern times is that of Hume.[47] The depth of Hume's denial must be appreciated. He eliminates "cause" and "effect" as names of intelligible objects. He does not question the naturalness and appropriateness of the thoroughgoing certitude that things arise and can only arise through causes. He rather says that the source of the certitude is not knowledge, because causal connection is not a possible object of knowledge.[48] Furthermore, we

---

46.   In accordance with the text of St. Thomas being discussed (*De potentia* 5.1), I limit myself to the case of material substances: see ST 1.87.3 *ad* 1.

47.   See Hume, *Treatise* I.III.III (pp. 78-82).

48.   See Hume, in *The Letters of David Hume*, ed. J.Y.T. Greig, Oxford, Clarendon Press, 1932, I, 187: ". . . I have never asserted so absurd a Proposition as that *anything might arise without a cause*: I only maintained that our Certainty of the Falsehood of that Proposition proceeded neither from Intuition or Demonstration: but from another source" (quoted by Owens, "The Causal Proposition—Principle or Conclusion?", p. 170, n. 35). On the impossibility of causal connection as an object of knowledge, see Hume, *Treatise* I.III.XIV (p. 161): "Now nothing is more evident, than that the human mind cannot form such an idea of two objects, as to conceive any connexion betwixt them, or comprehend distinctly that power or efficacy, by which they are united." Ibid. (p. 166): ". . . the simple view of any two objects or actions, however related, can never give us any idea of power, or of a connexion betwixt them. . . ." I must admit that it seems to me that on Humean grounds we can hardly be said to have certainty of the falsehood of the proposition: something might arise without a cause. If anything, we would have certainty that it is not a proposition at all, not an intelligible discourse. No use of the word "cause" would seem to me acceptable, except as illustrative of unintelligibility. This I would say is because I regard the word "cause" as involving in its meaning the attribution of

must focus on the source of the strength of the Humean conviction. How can he be so sure of the impossibility of cause/effect being an object of knowledge? The source, I would say, is our appreciation of the diversity of one being from another. The key doctrine of Hume is that an effect is quite distinct from its cause. *The effect is not the cause.* [49] This is, of course, quite true, and most unambiguously true as regards efficient causality, which is the target of Hume's critique. However, it is taken as implying that from the idea of the effect, one can never arrive at a cause. One can envisage the effect without envisaging the cause. [50] Indeed, what would it be to envisage a connection? Hume stresses the "loose" character of all events, a looseness extending to every perception with respect to every other perception. [51]

What can one say to the Humean? It is true that an effect is not its cause. This is part of the truth expressed by the causal principle itself. An effect depends on something else, i.e., another thing. However, is an effect conceivable without its cause?

Suppose that the term "an effect" is taken to mean the effect of an efficient cause. Then it is naming primarily the *relation* by which one thing depends on another. [52] Looked at from the viewpoint of quiddity, looked at "logically" if one will, its whole notion is formed in function of the cause, i.e., that towards which it orders the thing which is the effect. Thus, if we mean by "the effect" the very relation to the cause, it cannot be conceived

---

real intelligible connexion to objects (see ibid., p. 168). Hume's redefining of "cause" seems to me quite beside the point.

49.   See Hume, *An Enquiry concerning Human Understanding* (EHU), IV.I (para. 25, p. 29): "For the effect is totally different from the cause. . . ." And ibid., p. 30: ". . . every effect is a distinct event from its cause."

50.   See Hume, *Treatise*, I.III.III (pp. 79-80): ". . . as all distinct ideas are separable from each other, and as the ideas of cause and effect are evidently distinct, 'twill be easy for us to conceive any object to be non-existent this moment and existent the next, without conjoining to it the distinct idea of a cause or productive principle. The separation, therefore, of the idea of a cause from that of a beginning of existence, is plainly possible for the imagination; and consequently the actual separation of these objects is so far possible, that it implies no contradiction nor absurdity . . ."

51.   See above, n. 7. See also *Treatise*, Appendix (pp. 634-636), especially: ". . . there are two principles, which I cannot render consistent [with, I take it, a satisfying theory of personal identity]; nor is it in my power to renounce either of them, viz. *that all our distinct perceptions are distinct existences*, and *that the mind never perceives any real connexion among distinct existences*" (p. 636, his italics). And again: ibid., I.IV.V (p. 233).

52.   See St. Thomas, *De potentia* 7.9. *ad* 4. I have been taking it for granted that "effect of efficient cause" signifies primarily a relation. For this corresponds to St.Thomas's doctrine, especially CM 5.17.1003-1005 and 1026-1029. One of the three modes of relation is of the measurable to the measure, not according to quantity, but measure of *esse* and *veritas* (1003). He explains: "Ordinatur autem una res ad aliam . . . secundum esse, prout esse unius rei dependet ab alia, et sic est tertius modus . . ." (1004) He comes back to this doctrine in 1027, at the end: ". . . ab eo quaelibet res mensuratur, a quo ipsa dependet." Notice that this is quite a distinct conception from action and passion as relatives.

without the cause.[53] However, there are two things to note about this conception. One is that the name of any predicamental accident signifies primarily the accident itself, and only secondarily the subject of the accident, i.e., the substance in which it inheres.[54] Thus, already, on this basis, the thing which is the effect, the thing which has order through the accidental relation, is somewhat out of the picture, when one says: "an effect depends on its cause." One is not speaking to any great extent about what sort of thing is characterized as an effect. In this way, we already see some truth in the Humean contention that one can dissociate the notions of effect and cause. It is rather that effect gets split up into an item associated with cause and an item dissociated from cause. And one might make this same point starting from the side of the substance. A substance must be considerable without considering any accident (that is not to admit that any substance other than God can *be actually* in dissociation from all accidents).[55]

However, secondly, we must note a special feature of relation, which distinguishes it from other types of accident. The other types of accident, such as quantity and quality, include the substance in which they inhere in the proper quidditative notion of the accident. Quantity is the quantity *of the* substance, quality the quality *of the* substance. Relation, on the other hand, is a type of notion peculiarly devoid of quidditative content of its own. Its intrinsic notion is the "towards," faced entirely towards its term, its goal, and more *associated with* the thing it relates than inherent in or conceived as "of" the thing it relates. A real relation *is inherent* in the thing it relates, but its quidditative content does not include that inherence.[56] This means that, more than in the case of any other sort of accident, it is true of relation, and so of the relation which is signified by "an effect," that it says nothing about the thing in which it is. Thus, in this way also, Hume's contention makes sense, that one can think of an effect without thinking of its cause. That is, "relation to a cause" says peculiarly little about what kind of thing it is to which it properly belongs.

Still, we have not as yet addressed the question (is an effect conceivable without its cause?) in the most appropriate way. We have stayed at the level of form or quiddity, considered quite abstractly. While the object of the

53. This is the sense of "an effect depends on its cause" (an effect must have a cause, presupposes a cause, since they are correlatives) which Hume rightly (at least in a way) says cannot resolve the question: is a thing which begins to exist, an effect?

54. See St. Thomas, CM 5.9.894, where he criticizes Avicenna for not having seen this point.

55. See St. Thomas, *Quodl.* 10.2.1: ". . . de re aliqua possumus loqui dupliciter: uno modo secundum quod est in rerum natura; alio modo secundum quod est in consideratione nostra. Primo modo accipitur substantia rei cum omnibus suis dispositionibus et operationibus, quia sine his substantia non invenitur in rerum natura; sed secundo modo potest accipi substantia absque suis dispositionibus, quia consideratio substantiae non dependet a consideratione suarum dispositionum."

56. See St. Thomas, ST 1.28.2 (188a38-b15); and ibid., *ad* 2; also *Quodl.* 11.2.1. and CM 4.1.539-543.

intellect is form, quiddity, or nature, the intellect (and not merely the senses) knows also the being actually (the *esse*) and the mode of *esse proper* to the nature. As St. Thomas says:

> . . . the intellect knows the stone according to the intelligible *esse* which it has in the intellect, but nevertheless it [also] knows the *esse* of the stone in [its, the stone's] proper nature.[57]

This it knows first of all in its operation of composing and dividing.[58] However, it does not merely *encounter* the sensible existence of things, but conducts itself *as intellect* with respect to such existence, i.e., discerns, to the extent possible, *what* existence *is*, and *what is* the proper mode of existence of the sensible natures. As St. Thomas says:

> . . . the sense knows *esse* only as developed in the here and now, but the intellect apprehends *esse* absolutely and according to all time.[59]

In fact, there is a sequence of intelligible objects natural to the human intellect, according as there is a unity and sequence of intelligible features to be found in things. A form has its proper mode of being. When one has grasped the form, one grasps, secondly, its mode of being *as proportionate to the form.*[60]

Thus, first, we note the primacy for intellection of the grasp of quiddity or specific nature as such. This is the *"ens"* which is the object of the intellect. Such form or essence is anything but existentially neutral. It is *intrinsically* "principle of being" (*principium essendi*).[61] Through it, *esse* is already known

---

57. See ST 1.14.6 *ad* 1 (98a20-24).
58. See ST 1.14.14 *ad* 2: ". . . compositio enuntiabilis significat aliquod esse rei . . ." (Ottawa ed. has "aliquid," seemingly a misprint). See also ST 1.16.1 and 3: ". . . esse rei, non veritas eius, causat veritatem intellectus . . ." and ST 1.16.2: ". . . quando iudicat rem ita se habere sicut est forma quam de re apprehendit, tunc primo cognoscit et dicit verum. Et hoc facit componendo et dividendo; nam in omni propositione aliquam formam significatam per praedicatum, vel applicat alicui rei significatae per subiectum, vel removet ab ea."
59. See ST 1.75.6 (445b31-34).
60. See ST 1.85.5 (531b12-21): ". . . intellectus humanus non statim in prima apprehensione capit perfectam rei cognitionem; sed primo apprehendit aliquid de ipsa, puta quidditatem ipsius rei, quae est primum et proprium obiectum intellectus; et deinde intelligit proprietates et accidentia et habitudines circumstances rei essentiam. Et secundum hoc necesse habet unum apprehensum alii componere et dividere . . . ." Concerning the mode of being of the form or nature, see ST 1.5.5: ". . . Praeexigitur autem ad formam determinatio sive commensuratio principiorum, seu materialium, seu efficientium ipsam: et hoc significatur per modum . . . ." Concerning the knowing of matter only according to its proportion to form, see ST 1.87.1 (540a31-36): ". . . intellectus manifestum est quod, inquantum est cognoscitivus rerum materialium, non cognoscit nisi quod est actu; et inde est quod non cognoscit materiam primam nisi secundum proportionem ad formam . . . ."
61. See ST 1-2.85.6 (1181b4-11): ". . . corruptiones et defectus rerum sunt naturales, non quidem secundum inclinationem formae, quae est principium essendi et perfectionis, sed secundum inclinationem materiae, quae proportionaliter attribuitur tali formae secundum distributionem universalis agentis . . . ." See also ST 1.75.6 (445b2-6): "Esse autem per se convenit formae, quae est actus. Unde materia secundum hoc acquirit esse in actu, quod acquirit formam; secundum hoc autem accidit in ea corruptio, quod separatur forma ab ea."

"in principle." Secondly, this principle is applied to the consideration of things as sensed and imagined, that is, to things as they exist. Thus, the intellect sees the existence of the thing as flowing from the principle, i.e., sees formal causality, and sees the *unity* of the principle with the mode of being, sees the "fit." Thus, St. Thomas can say:

> There are many modes of being of things. For there are some [things], the nature of which has being only in 'this individual matter': and of this mode are all corporeal [things]. . . . .[62]

This is a universal, necessary judgment about the mode of being proper to a certain sort of nature. It is an assessment of the *per se* unity of the *concrete* substance. It sees the nature as "at home" in the concrete, the principle of being *of* the concrete, and so as *presupposing* the individual matter; indeed, as presupposing even the efficient cause.[63]

I am going into this issue because it seems to me that the proposition "an effect depends on its cause" belongs properly to the same order of discourse as the statements about the mode of being proper to corporeal things. This order of discourse coincides, I suggest, with what St. Thomas calls, when commenting upon Aristotle, the consideration of "being as it is divided by act and potency," which consideration is wider than that which focuses on being as divided by the categories. The latter is a division of perfect being, whereas the former includes both the perfect and the imperfect.[64] "An effect depends on its cause" expresses, first of all, the dependence of the composite of matter and form with respect to its form. It expresses, secondly, the dependence of the composite of matter and form on the source of the form. It expresses, thirdly, the dependence of the composite of matter and form on

---

62. See ST 1.12.4 (64b13-17): "Est autem multiplex modus essendi rerum. Quaedam enim sunt, quorum natura non habet esse nisi in hac materia individuali; et huiusmodi sunt omnia corporalia . . . ."
63. See above, n. 60, T 1.5.5. It seems to me that, for this doctrine of our conception of the mode of being proper to corporeal natures, CM 7.11, the entire *lectio*, is of interest. The conception of the common matter, included in the species or quiddity of the thing, is a kind of bridge, intelligibly, from the substantial form to the individual matter. We might also remember that the nature and the mode of being together constitute a *per se* unity: see ST 1.29.1 (192a20-21): "Substantia enim individuatur per seipsam . . . ." For our knowledge of the modes of being of forms, we should remember ST 1.84.1 (512a45-b7), and also *Quaestiones de anima* 20, *ad* 1 *sed contra* (ed. Robb, p. 262): sense knowledge also constitutes a medium for the intellect in forming its conception of things existing concretely. And see also Cajetan's commentary on ST 1.84 7 (521b44-22a14), to be found in the Leonine ed. of ST, *ad loc.*
64. See St. Thomas, CM 5.9.889: ". . . distinguit [Aristoteles] ens, quod est extra animam, per decem praedicamenta, quod est ens perfectum . . . dividit ens per potentiam et actum: et ens sic divisum est communius quam ens perfectum. Nam ens in potentia, est ens secundum quid tantum et imperfectum . . . ." One is talking about the *proportion* of the contingent to the necessary, one is using the *light* which the necessary throws on the contingent: an effect depends on its cause, or act is prior to potency. See ST 1.87.1 (quoted above, n. 60); also ST 1.86.3 and 1.79.9 ad 3. See also CM 9.5.1826-1829, on the role of *proportion* in the grasping of act and potency.

the goal which the agent, the source of the form, has in view. All of these things come into sight precisely inasmuch as one views things from the viewpoint of *esse*; as St. Thomas says: "Something is called 'caused' because it has a cause of its *esse*."[65]

Can one conceive of the effect without the cause? This question primarily means: can one think of the effect *as having being* without the cause *having being*? Can one think of the composite of matter and form without the form? (Or, can one think of the matter having being without the form?)[66] And can one think of the composite of matter and form as existing without an efficient cause?[67] To the extent that one has caught sight of the existing thing as a composite, i.e., as distinct items which nevertheless are so proportioned one to another as together to constitute a kind of *per se* unit, one is seeing the need for the causes. One is seeing the dependence.[68]

---

65.   See above, n. 26.

66.   See *De potentia* 4.1; ST 1.66.1; *Quodl.* 3.1.1: "Omne enim quod est actu: vel est ipse actus, vel est potentia participans actum. Esse autem actu [I suggest reading: actum] repugnat rationi materiae, quae secundum propriam rationem est ens in potentia. Relinquitur ergo quod non possit esse in actu nisi in quantum participat actum. Actus autem participatus a materia nihil est aliud quam forma; unde idem est dictu, materiam esse in actu, et materiam habere formam. Dicere ergo quod materia sit in actu sine forma, est dicere contradictoria esse simul; unde a Deo fieri non potest."

67.   It is precisely the negative answer to this question which leads St. Thomas to an ultimate conclusion of the divine conservational causality, in the text which has constituted our starting point in this paper: *De potentia* 5.1, and its parallels (ST 1.104.1, etc). This doctrine of our appreciation of the need for a cause necessarily involves our grasping of form as form, i.e., as something which according to its own nature transcends the material individual. In contrast to form so seen (i.e., in its proper amplitude or ontological wealth), it is then seen, according to its presence in matter, as diminished form, secondary form, form derived from form existing in a higher mode of being: see ST 1.3.8: "Tertio, quia nulla pars compositi potest esse simpliciter prima in entibus; neque etiam materia et forma, quae sunt primae partes compositorum. Nam materia est in potentia, potentia autem est posterior actu simpliciter . . . . Forma autem quae est pars compositi, est forma participata; sicut autem participans est posterius eo quod est per essentiam, ita et ipsum participatum; sicut ignis in ignitis est posterius eo quod est per essentiam." We see how the sensible experience of fire as "at home" in one thing and as merely "present through the influence" in the next thing leads us to the notion of derivative form. See also our paper referred to in n. 28, as well as our forthcoming paper "St. Thomas, Joseph Owens and Existence" (*New Scholasticism*, Fall, 1982).

68.   Hume, *Treatise* I.III.III (*ed. cit.*, p. 79), speaking of the proposition "whatever begins to exist must have a cause of its existence," says: "all certainty arises from the comparison of ideas, and from the discovery of such relations as are unalterable, so long as the ideas continue the same. These relations are *resemblance, proportions of quantity and number, degrees of any quality, and contrariety*; none of which are imply'd in this proposition, *Whatever has a beginning has also a cause of existence*. That proposition therefore is not intuitively certain" (his italics). See St. Thomas, *De substantiis separatis* c. 7, lines 47-52 (*Opera omnia* t. 40, Rome 1969: Ad Sanctae Sabinae): "Manifestum est autem quod cum ens per potentiam et actum dividatur, quod actus est potentia perfectior et *magis habet de ratione essendi*; non enim simpliciter esse dicimus quod est in potentia, sed solum quod est actu" (my italics). I would say that the conception of "whatever begins to exist" includes the conception of the not-being *of the thing*; and that this conception necessarily involves that of the thing's being in potency (see ST 1.14.9). Thus, I see the Humean proposition as a consideration of degrees of a quality, taking quality in the large

To return to Hume, perhaps we could say that the problem he poses occurs because he requires that all intellectual knowledge be in the purely quidditative order, whereas cause and effect are intelligible objects but not the intelligible objects that occur first in our order of objects.

---

sense of a communicable formal perfection; it amounts to saying that that which in its own nature is a being in potency has actual being only from another. It is the discerning of a necessary relation or proportion between intelligibles. See also above, n. 52, on measure and the measurable.

La sixième voie de Maritain et la philosophie moderne de Dieu

M. l'abbé Stanislaw Kowalczyk
Université catholique de Lublin

My paper consists of three parts. The first is a statement of the formulation of the sixth way. Maritain distinguished between two steps in the argument: pre-philosophical and philosophical. Man intuitively experiences his own cogito—*the intellect's activity. He thus becomes aware of the spirituality of the human person. The knowing subject cannot arise out of the natural evolution of the material world or of the biocosmos. The transphenomenal subjectivity of the human mind cannot be fully explained except in absolute personal thinking, that is, in God.*

The second part of the paper discusses the problem of the genesis of the sixth way. The central element of the argument is the affirmation cogito, ergo semper fui, *which is related to Descartes'* cogito. *Now, Descartes'* cogito *was a continuation of Saint Augustine's* cogito. *Therefore we must recognize the author of the* Confessions *as the precursor of Maritain's sixth way. The starting point of Saint Augustine's philosophy of God is the world of the human person. The Thomist Maritain also shows the influence of Descartes and Henri Bergson. Maritain has re-interpreted Descartes'* cogito *in such a way that for him the* cogito *is not only an act of thinking but also a thinking being.*

The third and last part of the paper considers the value of the argument. Maritain was a fervent and consistent Thomist; however, his Thomism was open. The sixth way forms a transition from the cosmological to the anthropological argument within the frame of theodicy but, at the same time, it forms an important link between existential Thomism and phenomenological Thomism. Maritain aimed at broadening the Thomist philosophy of God and this is why he refers to internal experience as tied to man's psychic world.

Le penseur catholique français Jacques Maritain (1882-1973) est appelé souvent « un maître pour notre temps[1] ». Ce qualificatif est actuel non seulement dans le domaine de la philosophie sociale, où le philosophe était précurseur du IIe concile du Vatican, mais aussi dans le domaine de la métaphysique. La célèbre sixième voie, constituant un des éléments originaux de la philosophie de l'auteur des *Approches de Dieu*, en est la manifestation. En vue d'étudier le rôle que joue la sixième voie de Maritain dans la théologie naturelle moderne, nous allons analyser successivement sa formulation, sa genèse, ainsi que sa valeur.

1. LA FORMULATION DE LA SIXIÈME VOIE

Notre but n'est pas l'analyse détaillée de la sixième voie de Maritain, car ceci constitue l'objet d'un article publié en 1980 dans la revue *Divus Thomas*[2]. Il ne s'agit ici que d'esquisser cet argument.

Dans la sixième voie, Maritain a fait une distinction entre deux étapes : la préphilosophique et la philosophique. Tout en remarquant une divergence entre ces deux étapes sur le plan épistémologico-méthodologique, il ne voyait

---

1. J. DAUJAT, *Maritain. Un maître pour notre temps*, Paris, 1979.
2. S. KOWALCZYK, *Le rôle de la sixième voie de J. Maritain dans la philosophie moderne de Dieu*, Divus Thomas, n° 84, 1980, pp. 381-393.

cependant pas de divergence essentielle dans les constatations portant sur le fond du problème. Il associait la certitude de l'existence de Dieu déjà à la première étape, basée sur l'intuition spontanée. L'homme vit intuitivement son propre *cogito* — l'activité de l'intellect. C'est de cette façon qu'il prend conscience de « la spiritualité naturelle de l'esprit » humain[3]. L'homme est un être « occupé à penser » : il est doté de la faculté d'auto-réflexion, il est conscient de ses propres expériences et de ses actions, il pose des questions et cherche la vérité. L'expérience existentielle du *cogito* lui permet de se voir possesseur d'une âme immatérielle.

> Nous possédons — écrivait Maritain — une expérience véritable de l'existence individuelle de notre âme, par quoi je comprends la connaissance de ses actions, c'est pourquoi la notion de notre *soi* est une notion fondée sur l'expérience[4].

Selon cette interprétation, l'intuition ne se limite pas à la sphère théorique de la réflexion de l'intellect, mais elle est conçue comme une expérience personnelle de la totalité de la personne humaine. Le fait de penser constitue la donnée universelle et directe de l'expérience de l'homme. La négation du fait de penser entraîne d'une façon inévitable une contradiction : tout en niant la pensée, nous nous en servons tout de même.

Pour Maritain, le *cogito* s'identifie à l'*existo*, car il n'y a pas de pensée sans existence réelle. C'est pourquoi Maritain concluait que l'activité cognitive intellectuelle de l'homme témoigne de son autonomie existentielle par rapport au monde de la matière. Si donc les paramètres de l'esprit humain et ceux de la matière sont hétérogènes, la pensée humaine ne peut pas être un produit matériel naturel. Le cosmos matériel ne peut pas donner l'explication adéquate de la genèse du phénomène de la pensée. La pensée témoigne de l'existence préalable d'un sujet pensant. *Cogito ergo semper fui.* La quintessence des analyses de l'auteur se résume dans l'énoncé suivant :

> J'ai toujours existé, moi qui pense, et non pas plus d'une existence ou d'une vie impersonnelle (sans personnalité pas de pensée [...]) donc d'une existence ou d'une vie suprapersonnelle. Où donc ? Il faut que ce soit dans un être à la personnalité transcendante en qui se trouvait d'une façon suréminente tout ce qu'il y a comme perfection sans ma pensée et dans toute pensée[5].

La pensée humaine existait donc en Dieu transcendant personnel, et c'est de l'existence de ce Dieu qu'est issue l'existence de l'homme.

Cette constatation termine l'étape préphilosophique de la sixième voie. L'étape suivante — philosophique — n'apporte pas de thèses nouvelles, mais elle constitue plutôt une confirmation du savoir acquis intuitivement par la voie de la motivation philosophique. Maritain a fait remarquer que l'activité de l'esprit humain n'est liée à la matière et à ses catégories — temps, espace, successivité des processus — qu'extérieurement et fonctionnellement. La pensée

---

3. J. MARITAIN, *Approches de Dieu*, Paris, p. 82.
4. *Id.*, Paris 1932, p. 883.
5. *Id.*, *Approches de Dieu*, p. 85.

ayant une dimension spirituelle, elle n'est donc pas soumise à la catégorie du temps : « Ce qui est spirituel n'est pas soumis au temps. Le lien propre du spirituel est au-dessus de l'existence temporelle[6] ».

L'élément suivant de l'analyse métaphysique de Maritain, c'est l'appel que celui-ci fait à l'adage : *actiones sunt suppositorum*. Les actions, y compris les actions humaines, sont étroitement liées au sujet dans lequel elles se déroulent. L'activité intellectuelle est liée à la conscience, et celle-ci, comme son fondement, a toujours besoin d'un être personnel. L'homme est un être à deux aspects : le matériel et le spirituel. Son *soi* matériel naît dans le temps et se détruit au moment de la mort. En tant que possesseur de la pensée réflexive, l'homme constitue le « centre d'activité spirituelle et capable de vivre ou d'exister de la sur-existence immatérielle[7] ». Le *soi* matériel de l'homme, sa matière et ses énergies physico-chimiques, préexistait dans la nature. Le *soi* pensant de l'homme ne peut pas venir du cosmos matériel, « Car l'esprit ne peut venir que d'un esprit, la pensée ne peut provenir que d'une pensée, donc d'une existence supérieure au temps[8] ». Le *soi* pensant spirituel de l'homme est donc transcendant au temps et à la matière.

C'est ici qu'apparaît la conclusion des considérations du philosophe français. Seul un autre être personnel, doué de la faculté de réflexion, et en même temps autonome dans sa durée, peut constituer la présource ontique de l'homme pensant. Dieu est un « acte de la pensée pure, de laquelle provient toute pensée[9] ». Le *soi* spirituel de l'homme a toujours existé en Dieu, non d'une façon formelle et personnelle, mais virtuelle et ontique. En tant qu'être pensant et conscient de lui-même, l'homme est à « l'image de Dieu ». C'est pourquoi, en dépit de toutes sortes de restrictions et de défauts existentiels, il participe à la vie suprapersonnelle de Dieu.

2.   LA GENÈSE DE LA SIXIÈME VOIE

L'argument de Maritain est devenu l'objet de différentes controverses[10]. Il y a des auteurs qui le discutent sans prendre de position doctrinale envers lui, il y en a d'autres qui portent sur lui un jugement favorable, d'autres encore qui le désapprouvent, entièrement ou en partie. Quant à nous, c'est l'attitude modérément critique qui nous paraît la plus juste. La plupart des auteurs passent sous silence le problème de la genèse historico-doctrinale de la sixième voie, ce qui rend plus difficile l'interprétation et l'évaluation de cet argument.

Jacques Maritain était un thomiste fervent, mais il interprétait le thomisme comme une philosophie qui s'ouvre à chaque nouvelle vérité, qu'elle soit

---

6.   *Ibid.*, p. 87.
7.   *Ibid.*, p. 88.
8.   *Ibid.*, pp. 88-89.
9.   *Ibid.*, p. 90.
10.   S. KOWALCZYK, art. cit., pp. 385-389.

découverte avant ou après saint Thomas d'Aquin. Pour lui, le thomisme était une philosophie progressive, constamment créatrice et véritablement réaliste. C'est pourquoi, à côté des cinq voies traditionnelles de l'Aquinate, l'auteur des *Approches de Dieu* en a formulé une sixième. Et bien que celle-ci se réfère au *cogito* de Descartes, elle comprend en même temps des filiations doctrinales bien antérieures. Sans doute c'est un argument d'inspiration augustinienne. L'attitude de Maritain à l'égard de saint Augustin n'étant pas dépourvue de sens critique, il se montre distant envers la métaphysique de *la vie interne* et de *la conversion* augustinienne[11]. Cependant Maritain était contre les tentatives d'opposer saint Augustin à saint Thomas. Il était persuadé que ce dernier parachevait le premier même au plan de la théodicée. La preuve en est qu'entre autres l'argument de la vérité de saint Augustin a été repris d'une façon créatrice dans la quatrième voie. En voyant en saint Thomas l'héritier de la pensée augustinienne, Maritain s'en inspirait visiblement. Sa conception de l'intuition, organiquement liée à l'expérience intérieure de l'homme, en fait preuve.

L'élément central de la sixième voie, c'est l'affirmation : *cogito ergo semper fui*. Le *cogito* de Descartes s'inspirait du *cogito* de l'auteur des *Confessions*. Les deux penseurs partageaient le même désir de découvrir des vérités indubitables; les deux comptaient parmi les vérités de cette sorte le phénomène de la pensée, saisi dans le phénomène du doute. Cette analogie n'exclut pourtant pas de différences importantes entre eux. Chez Descartes, l'évidence du *cogito* est liée à la théorie du nativisme, tandis que saint Augustin se prononçait conséquemment pour le réalisme épistémologique. Descartes prenait pour point de départ le fait de la pensée, dans laquelle il trouvait la confirmation de la réalité de l'homme. Augustin mettait l'accent sur la simultanéité de la connaissance des trois niveaux existentiels de l'homme : existence, vie et pensée[12]. Il ne déduisait pas la réalité de l'existence du fait de la pensée, mais c'est dans le sujet pensant qu'il remarquait le fait de l'existence. Le *cogito* augustinien, bien qu'éloigné du courant de la philosophie aristotélicienne, ne s'opposait pas au réalisme épistémologique. C'est pourquoi il faut reconnaître l'évêque d'Hippone comme précurseur de la sixième voie de Maritain, car dans sa philosophie de Dieu, il prenait comme point de départ le monde de la personne humaine.

C'est aussi sans doute la philosophie moderne et contemporaine, avec Descartes en tête, qui a exercé une influence sensible sur la définition de l'argument du thomiste français. L'auteur du *Paysan de la Garonne* a formulé à l'adresse de Descartes une série d'objections importantes : idéalisme, idéosophie — insistance sur la philosophie des mots et non sur celle des êtres,

---

11. J. MARITAIN, *Distinguer pour unir ou les degrés du savoir*, p. 593; voir aussi pp. 600-606.
12. Saint Augustin, *De libero arbitrio*, 2,3,7 PL 32, 1243.

formulation de pseudo-problèmes et de pseudo-solutions[13]. L'acuité de ces objections ne met cependant pas en question le fait que le *cogito ergo sum* est voisin du *cogito ergo semper fui* de Maritain[14]. Cela ne signifie pourtant pas que les philosophes pensent de façon identique; ils se distinguent souvent aussi bien dans leur ontologie que dans leur gnoséologie. Le thomiste français se prononçait contre la séparation du *logos* d'avec l'être. Le *cogito*, ce n'est pas seulement un acte de la pensée, mais un être pensant. La perception de l'être est même antérieure à celle de la pensée. La réinterprétation du *cogito* de Descartes, visible chez Maritain, a probablement été inspirée par le *cogito* de saint Augustin.

Le thomisme existentiel de Maritain diffère d'une façon considérable de l'existentialisme moderne, énoncé par Soren Kierkegaard. Mettre en relief l'acte d'existence dans la structure de l'être ne veut pas dire concentrer l'attention sur l'existence conçue comme la durée de l'homme. Malgré cela, le thomiste français a convenu que les deux courants de l'existentialisme se rejoignent par la mise en valeur du rôle de l'intuition cognitive de l'existence[15]. Tandis que dans le domaine de l'ontologie Maritain admettait l'existentialisme dans le sens du thomisme classique, dans sa sixième voie, il s'est rapproché de l'existentialisme moderne, quoique qu'il ait associé celui-ci à la conception de l'homme de saint Thomas.

Chez cet auteur français nous remarquons aussi l'influence d'Henri Bergson à qui Maritain devait avant tout son abandon du scientisme. Plus tard, en tant que thomiste, il jugeait défavorablement la pensée philosophique de Bergson, en lui reprochant la séparation de l'intuition d'avec l'intellect, la dépréciation de la connaissance intellectuelle au profit de la sphère instinctive et émotionnelle, le jugement exagérément critique de la valeur cognitive des notions, enfin la sympathie passagère pour le panthéisme[16]. Cette critique sévère n'empêche pas que l'auteur des *Approches de Dieu* est resté sous l'influence de Bergson jusqu'à la fin de sa vie. C'est grâce à Bergson qu'il a appris le respect du concret, qu'il a valorisé l'expérience dans le sens large du mot, qu'il a reconnu le rôle directeur de l'intuition dans le domaine de la philosophie, qu'il s'est intéressé enfin au phénomène de la variabilité du monde. C'est à la même influence que Maritain devait son éloignement du thomisme spéculatif et académique, l'élargissement de la base épistémologico-méthodologique de la philosophie, enfin la concentration de l'attention sur le rôle de l'intuition. Dans son épistémologie, l'auteur des *Degrés du savoir* [...] rompt avec le schématisme du thomisme traditionnel, en reconnaissant le pluralisme des types de connaissance humaine et celui des méthodes scientifiques. La sixième voie en est une confirmation nette.

---

13. J. MARITAIN, *Le paysan de la Garonne*, Paris, 1966, pp. 150-152.
14. J. BOBIK, *The Sixth Way, The Modern Schoolman*, 1974, n° 2, p. 105.
15. J. MARITAIN, *Raison et raisons*, Paris 1947, pp. 96-97.
16. *Id.*, *Le paysan de la Garonne*, pp. 205-206.

3.   LA VALEUR DE LA SIXIÈME VOIE

La sixième voie de Maritain, malgré certains éléments controversés, a une grande importance pour la philosophie moderne de Dieu. Cette importance consiste surtout dans le fait que le thomisme a valorisé la connaissance existentielle et intuitive et l'expérience anthropologique dans le domaine de la théodicée.

Le thomisme classique reconnaissait toujours la nécessité absolue de l'intuition dans l'argumentation en faveur de l'existence de Dieu, mais d'habitude il limitait son rôle à l'assertion des lois fondamentales de l'être et de la pensée (*prima principia*). Le thomiste français a considérablement élargi le rôle de l'intuition dans la voie cognitive vers Dieu. En principe, il n'a jamais donné de description adéquate de l'intuition, en se contentant de la caractéristique de ce phénomène selon ses différents aspects. La notion d'« intuition » étant sémantiquement proche de celle de *vision*, l'intuition c'est avant tout la perception visuelle — une saisie très immédiate. Il existe aussi l'intuition intellectuelle, qui est la connaissance intellectuelle non discursive, directe, ayant lieu sans l'intermédiaire du raisonnement[17]. Le contraire de la connaissance intuitive, c'est la connaissance indirecte. Maritain a distingué une double connaissance indirecte — objective, liée au raisonnement discursif, et subjective, se manifestant par exemple au cours de la construction des notions et de certains jugements[18]. Ce n'est que cette première qui est en opposition avec la connaissance intuitive, c'est pourquoi nous pouvons parler de *l'intuition abstraite*[19]. La connaissance intuitive n'exclut pas de simples actes cognitifs comme la généralisation, l'abstraction, l'analyse, la comparaison, etc.

Le thomiste français a distingué plusieurs genres de connaissance intuitive. Il a attribué l'intuition, conçue au sens strict, à Dieu, qui se passe de l'intermédiaire des impressions, des notions et des conclusions. Au stade de sa vie terrestre, l'homme prend connaissance, d'une façon intuitive et avec son intellect, de l'existence de l'être et de son propre *soi*[20]. Il n'est pas clair qu'il s'agisse de deux types différents d'intuition ou bien d'une double fonction de la même intuition. Néanmoins, Maritain liait l'intuition de l'être à celle de la subjectivité du sujet humain en tant que personne. Il parlait également de l'intuition du beau, du bien, du sacrum, etc. C'était donc une interprétation personnaliste de l'intuition.

En remarquant le rôle directeur de l'intuition dans la philosophie de Dieu, Maritain parlait de la connaissance préphilosophique de Dieu[21]. Il était

---

17.   *Id., Sept leçons sur l'être et les premiers principes de la raison spéculative*, Paris, 1934, p. 54.
18.   *Id., La philosophie bergsonienne*, Paris 1948, pp. 34 *sqq*.
19.   Voir F. MURAWIEC, *Rola intuicji w przyjmowaniu zakiżeń w metafizyce ogólnej u J. Maritaina* (Rôle de l'intuition dans l'acceptation des premiers principes dans la métaphysique générale de J. Maritain), Varsovie 1974, surtout pp. 25-35.
20.   J. MARITAIN, *Approches de Dieu*, p. 12.
21.   *Ibid.*, pp. 9-23.

convaincu que l'esprit humain est capable de reconnaître la *présource* de tout être d'une façon spontanée et naturelle. La prise de conscience de la présence de Dieu ne résulte pas de la motivation philosophique, mais de la connaissance intuitive. Or l'homme, en éprouvant la fragilité de sa propre existence, reconnaît intuitivement l'existence de « l'être sans le néant », c'est-à-dire de Dieu. Toute la motivation philosophique de la réalité de Dieu, y compris les voies de saint Thomas d'Aquin, constitue « le développement et l'explication de la connaissance naturelle »; chaque raisonnement philosophique « est plongé dans l'intuition primitive de l'existence[22] ». De cette façon toute la théodicée s'appuie sur l'intuition, dont le point final est la reconnaissance de Dieu en tant qu'être suprême, existant par lui-même[23].

C'est aussi la sixième voie de Maritain qui est organiquement liée à la connaissance existentielle et intuitive. En faisant distinction entre l'élément préphilosophique et philosophique de cet argument, l'auteur des *Approches de Dieu* a attribué la certitude de l'existence de Dieu à la connaissance préphilosophique, fondée sur l'intuition. Maritain était persuadé que c'est intuitivement que nous reconnaissons l'éternité de l'existence du *soi* humain et sa préexistence dans la nature de Dieu : « J'avais (mais sans pouvoir dire moi) une existence éternelle en Dieu avant de recevoir une existence temporelle dans ma propre nature et ma propre personnalité[24]. Cette constatation, résulte-t-elle de la connaissance intuitive? C'est là un des moments controversés de la sixième voie. Probablement Maritain attribue à l'intuition trop de pouvoir, à savoir la possibilité de connaître la préexistence de l'homme en Dieu. L'existence de l'homme dans les idées éternelles de Dieu constitue l'effet de la pensée philosophique discursive et non de l'expérience intuitive. Aussi il n'y a pas de doute qu'après Maritain, relativement à la philosophie de Dieu, nous ne pouvons plus nous limiter à la connaissance conceptuelle et discursive du thomisme traditionnel. Ce dernier type de connaissance n'épuise pas les possibilités et la richesse de la connaissance intellectuelle de l'homme. La conception de l'intuition de Maritain n'est pas toujours présentée clairement et sans ambiguïté, c'est pourquoi sa fonction dans la théodicée exige d'autres précisions.

La valeur de la sixième voie consiste aussi, ou plutôt avant tout, dans le fait qu'elle constitue le passage de l'argumentation cosmologique à l'argumentation anthropologique en faveur de l'existence de Dieu. C'est une nouveauté dans le courant du thomisme existentiel, dont elle constitue une réinterprétation et un élargissement. Ce n'était pourtant pas l'abandon du réalisme et l'acceptation de l'idéalisme et du subjectivisme, car la personne humaine, à tous ses niveaux existentiels et sous tous ses aspects, est un être réel. La réalité de l'homme ne se limite pas à la sphère du *soi* matériel, mais

---

22. *Ibid.*, pp. 18-19.
23. *Id.*, *Le paysan de la Garonne*, p. 199.
24. *Id.*, *Approches de Dieu*, pp. 85-86.

elle comprend aussi le *soi* pensant — immatériel, actif, révélateur. En recherchant Dieu, l'homme ne devrait pas omettre son univers intérieur : réflexion, sens, vérité, et conscience. Maritain l'a reconnu en formulant sa sixième voie. Ainsi, il a fondé la philosophie de Dieu sur l'expérience non seulement cosmologique, mais aussi anthropologique[25]. Le thomisme traditionnel, en décrivant l'homme surtout selon la terminologie aristotélicienne (acte — puissance, matière — forme, essence — existence) ne rend pas d'une façon adéquate la spécificité de l'homme en tant que sujet et que personne. Le résultat en était la conception appauvrie de l'expérience, centrée sur la perception sensuelle. L'expérience de l'homme, née du contact avec le cosmos matériel, n'épuise pas toute la richesse du vécu. À côté de l'expérience anthropologique, provoquée par le dialogue de l'homme avec l'univers des personnes, et dont la forme fondamentale est la conscience de son propre *soi*.

En formulant sa sixième voie, Maritain s'est référé avant tout au phénomène de l'*auto-conscience* et à l'expérience de la pensée humaine. Les expériences de ce genre constituent la reconnaissance intuitive de la spiritualité du *soi* de la personne humaine. La réflexion philosophique suivante indique que l'être spirituel ne peut être issu que d'un autre être spirituel — autonome et tout-puissant. Ainsi, ce n'est que Dieu qui peut être la cause définitive de l'homme. Le sujet pensant, la personne, ne peut pas être le résultat de l'évolution naturelle du monde matériel, ou bien celle du *biocosmos*. L'affirmation que la pensée ne vient que de la pensée et que l'esprit n'est qu'un produit de l'esprit, est l'élément fondamental de la sixième voie. La thèse, quant à son fond, est juste, quoique la motivation du penseur français ne soit ni complète ni entièrement claire.

En faisant appel dans la sixième voie à l'expérience anthropologique, l'auteur en question adhère au courant de la philosophie augustinienne. Saint Augustin prouvait l'existence de Dieu en se référant au phénomène de la connaissance de la vérité, lié organiquement au domaine de la pensée humaine. Blaise Pascal, en qualifiant l'homme de « roseau pensant », voulait exprimer que la transcendance existentielle de la personne humaine était liée au phénomène de la connaissance intellectuelle. De notre temps, c'est Maurice Blondel qui accentue le fait que le *logos* humain n'est pas une fonction du *bios*. Dans son interprétation la réflexion intellectuelle est une expérience de l'existence de Dieu, car la pensée et la vérité transcendent les dimensions du monde matériel.

L'expérience anthropologique, étant à la base de la sixième voie de Maritain, a été limitée au phénomène de la pensée. Dans la formulation de l'argument manque la référence à l'expérience axiologique, associée aux valeurs de la vérité, du bien, de la sainteté, du beau, etc. Pourtant, dans d'autres ouvrages, le thomiste français s'est référé à ce genre d'expérience et, même, il lui a attribué une fonction cognitive limitée par rapport au

---

25. Voir J. E. SMITH, *Experience and God*, New York, 1968.

problème de Dieu. Il écrivait plus d'une fois au sujet de la perception du beau, qui est « une inclination spirituelle vers Dieu, un commencement incertain [...] de la connaissance de Dieu[26] ». Il attachait aussi une grande importance à l'expérience morale, en reconnaissant les liens étroits de celle-ci avec l'assertion ou la négation de Dieu. Et bien qu'il n'ait pas formulé l'argument déontologique formel en faveur de la réalité de Dieu, il a remarqué tout de même sa corrélation organique avec l'option de la vision du monde[27]. Ce qui est particulièrement important, c'est « la dialectique intérieure du premier acte de volonté[28] ». En faisant un choix dans la hiérarchie des valeurs, en même temps, parfois inconsciemment, l'homme choisit Dieu ou bien le rejette. L'expérience re-ligieuse, et surtout mystique, est une autre forme de l'expérience axiologique[29]. Elles ne possèdent pas de caractère conceptuel et réflexif, mais elles constituent une expérience personnelle de la présence de Dieu. D'après Maritain, toute métaphysique vraiment importante comporte un élément de mysticisme, au moins *ex parte subjecti*. La connaissance philosophique trouve son couronnement dans la justification de la réalité de Dieu, la connaissance théologique, y compris la théologie cataphatique et la théologie anaphatique, se trouve finalement face à un mystère. C'est pourquoi l'expérience religieuse et mystique en est un complément précieux. Les relations des mystiques ne constituent pas un argument formel de l'existence de Dieu, mais un témoignage existentiel d'une expérience de *sa présence*[30].

Quand il référait aux expériences morale, artistique et religieuse, Maritain ne les incluait pas dans la structure de la sixième voie, ce qui appauvrit incontestablement celle-ci. Sans doute voulait-il rester fidèle au thomisme, et c'est pourquoi il parlait de l'expérience menant à l'assertion de Dieu, en renonçant à l'appellation d'« argument ». Seul le phénomène de la pensée a été reconnu par lui comme la base de la motivation philosophique de la réalité de l'absolu, alors que, sans motiver sa position, il ne considérait les autres formes de l'expérience axiologique que comme la reconnaissance existentielle de la présence de Dieu. Dans sa théodicée, Maritain a fait appel à l'univers de la personne humaine, mais seulement certains éléments de l'activité de celle-ci ont été reconnus par lui comme le fondement des arguments rationnels et métaphysiques de l'existence de la divinité. Ainsi il s'est arrêté à mi-chemin entre le thomisme traditionnel et le courant phénoménologico-augustinien de la pensée chrétienne.

Pour conclure nos réflexions, il faut constater que le rôle de la sixième voie de Maritain dans la philosophie moderne de Dieu est important pour plusieurs raisons. Tout d'abord l'argument proposé est, dans ses éléments essentiels, foncièrement juste. Si le monde de la matière a besoin d'une cause

---

26. J. MARITAIN, *Approches de Dieu*, p. 97.
27. *Ibid.*, p. 103.
28. *Ibid.*, p. 104.
29. *Ibid.*, pp. 99-100.
30. *Ibid.*, pp. 114-119.

efficiente adéquate, il en est de même, à plus forte raison, pour le monde de la personne humaine. C'est un argument qui répond aux exigences du réalisme épistémologique. Son point de départ est celui du phénomène de la pensée, attribut inséparable de la personne humaine. Quoique, sous l'aspect psycho-logique, l'on puisse parler du caractère subjectif des émotions de l'homme, sous l'aspect ontologique, le domaine de l'activité de l'être humain constitue incontestablement une partie de la réalité. Cette réalité ne s'explique d'une manière adéquate qu'au moyen de la Pensée absolue et transcendante, c'est-à-dire à travers Dieu. Le point de départ de la sixième voie est l'homme, dans le visage spirituel duquel on peut remarquer, si on le désire vraiment, le reflet d'un *Autre*, c'est-à-dire la manifestation de la présence de Dieu. En éprouvant la transcendance de son être personnel, l'homme découvre dans son *soi* intérieur « le modèle intelligible ». Le rôle de l'intellect discursif dans la philosophie de Dieu, que nous ne pouvons certainement ni passer sous silence ni diminuer, consiste avant tout dans l'articulation des formes différentes de notre propre expérience. Si on l'oublie, les considérations sur la théodicée deviennent peu lisibles pour nos contemporains, qui apprécient l'expérience et le concret. Le mérite de Maritain est d'avoir revalorisé le rôle de l'expérience et de l'intuition dans le domaine de la philosophie de Dieu. C'est là la valeur principale de la sixième voie. Elle n'est certainement pas un nouveau canon, c'est pour cela qu'on peut, et qu'on doit, dépasser ses limites. Le thomiste français avait raison en associant l'argumentation cosmologique de la théodicée à l'argumentation anthropologique. Néanmoins, il faut regretter qu'il ait négligé dans sa philosophie de Dieu l'expérience axiologique sous ses différentes formes.

What Maritain Meant by "Abstractive Intuition"

MARY T. CLARK, R.S.C.J.
Manhattanville College, Purchase, N.Y.

Maritain employait l'expression « intuition abstractive » pour indiquer que la réalité est atteinte dans la connaissance. Le mot intuition se rapporte à l'immédiateté de la connaissance. Celle-ci est assurée par le caractère de ce qui a été abstrait de l'image sensible, à savoir les espèces impresse et expresse qui jouent le rôle de signes formels de la réalité physique. En tant que signes formels ou purs et à la différence des signes instrumentaux, ils font connaître d'une manière immédiate ce qu'ils représentent. Par ce moyen, l'intelligence atteint directement les aspects intelligibles de la réalité dans le concept. Ceci ne veut pas dire qu'il soit facile de connaître la nature complète d'une chose donnée; car l'expérience a un grand rôle à jouer. Ce processus implique deux réalités : l'objet connu spécifie la connaissance et l'intelligence atteint quelque chose d'autre qu'elle-même.

Bien que conscient du danger de confusion entre le terme intuition *pris dans le sens classique de connaissance par les sens et l'usage qu'il fait de ce terme, conscient aussi du mépris de plusieurs pour le terme* abstraction, *Maritain défend son expression comme le meilleur contraste qu'il puisse opposer aux erreurs de l'idéalisme moderne. Rejetant l'épistémologie de Descartes, de Kant et de Blondel, Maritain maintient que son explication du sens de la formule « intuition abstractive » établit la légitimité de l'épistémologie réaliste.*

Dans son explication de l'acte de connaître, Maritain est parfaitement conscient du problème critique. Fidèle à l'enseignement de saint Thomas d'Aquin et à celui de Jean de Saint-Thomas, il distingue soigneusement la relation entre l'esprit et la chose d'avec la relation entre la chose et l'esprit, la relation réelle et la relation de raison, montrant que l'acte de connaître ne change pas la chose connue. Ainsi Maritain semble justifié de se donner le qualificatif de « réaliste critique ».

The occasion for Jacques Maritain's philosophical explanation of his expression ''abstractive intuition'' was offered when certain critics reprehended him for saying that ''abstract knowledge immediately attains the real object in itself.''[1] Now the expression ''object attained *in se*'' signifies that a present and existing object causes knowledge without any go-between of image or representative idea. Maritain's answer to this charge against his was to answer that if a philosopher made such a statement, then that philosopher was confusing intellectual knowledge with sensitive knowledge. But he pleaded ''Not Guilty'' to the statement attributed to him. He then explained that he held that abstract knowledge ''attains the real itself'' (in a concept) and not the real ''in itself.''[2] Only in the Beatific Vision, asserts Maritain, does an intellect possess an object so immaterial that it sees it ''in itself.''

Because Maritain wanted to emphasize that reality is reached in knowledge, he chose to use the expression ''abstractive intuition.'' Sensible intuition terminates at an object taken as physically present. Conceptual knowledge, however, is of the object intentionally present. The addition of the word ''abstractive'' to ''intuition'' says precisely this. The possibility of reaching reality is due to the *means* of knowledge—the concept in its purity as a *formal*

---

1.   J. Maritain, *Réflexions sur l'intelligence* (3rd ed.), Paris, Desclée, 1930, p. 342.
2.   *Ibid.*

rather than an *instrumental* sign. An instrumental sign is itself first known before making known; a formal sign makes known before being itself known through reflection. A formal sign's whole nature is to signify. It is a living reference to something else; it is a sign in which a thing is immediately perceived. For in its role as a means *by which* or *in which* the real object is known, the concept in no way prevents the intellect from reaching its object immediately. It is accurate to say that nothing stands between abstract knowledge and the known object. This is because the concept is not a *quod* term but a term *in quo*.

The *quod* of intellectual apprehension—what is known—is *immediately* reached by the intellect in the concept. The concept is not an image or portrait of the thing nor an empty form; it is the very thing, but in the intellect the thing is essence or quiddity. Its state of existence is different. It existed individually and now exists universally. By an abstractive operation the intellect draws its object from the sensible datum and, thereby receiving its likeness or impressed species, from it produces a concept which it expresses to itself and in which it knows the thing in its non-temporal and necessary aspects. The essence receives its mode of existing from the mind but does not receive from the mind any of its intrinsic determinations. The one same essence exists in the mind and in the thing outside the mind. There is identity between being and thought but there is difference in their conditions. Through the senses a thing is known in its own existential conditions. Through the intellect a thing is abstracted from its own conditions and assumes the condition of immateriality and universality proper to mind. Whatever is received by a subject is received according to the conditions of the recipient.

We must therefore admit a certain disjunction between being and thought without forsaking their essential identity in the very act of knowing. This means that being and thought are not purely and simply the same thing. Parmenides thought they were, and Kant disjoins them absolutely. But for Maritain there is only a certain disjunction. Because the concept is purely form sign, the intellect becomes the object intentionally. The union takes place by the likeness or "vicar" of the object. This vicar is in the subject by the impressed and the expressed species, the prerequisite conditions for knowledge. The impressed species is the object as intentional "seed"; the expressed species or concept is the object as intentional "fruit." The likeness has two roles or functions. In the entitative order it is an accidental form, belonging to the subject, a mode of its thought; in the intentional order it is the thing itself as sign, the vicar of the reality being known, immaterially present to mind. The thing known exists intentionally in the knower and the knower becomes intentionally the thing known. When the mind is informed by the thing as "pure sign" and brings itself in act to a reality that is not limited to itself alone—there is "knowing."[3]

---

3. *Ibid.*, p. 63; J. Maritain, *The Degrees of Knowledge*, New York, Charles Scribner's Sons, 1959, pp. 116-117; Thomas Aquinas, *Contra Gentiles*, II.98; *De Veritate*, VIII.6. *ad* 3.

Maritain is not denying the need for sense knowledge when he states that abstract knowledge reaches the real, for the concept is the mind's response to the intellectual impressed species derived from the sensible object by the agent intellect. Nor when he says that by abstract knowledge we intuit the real is he denying the need for concepts (which have a mediate character). He is saying that we do not attain the object mediately in the sense that through another object the real object is known, but only through a formal sign whose purity ensures a most intimate and immediate union between the mind and the reality.

Two implications of this process are: the known object specifies knowledge, and the intellect reaches something other than itself. Otherwise, as St. Thomas was the first to note, all sciences would be reduced to psychology, and we would have the absurd situation where there would be no possibility of resolving contradictions.

Maritain has therefore used the expression "abstractive intuition" to emphasize the immediacy of human knowledge that must necessarily be abstracted from the sensible image. In using the word "intuition" he is aware of the danger. Yet he uses it quite apart from the way it was used by Kant and by scholastic philosophers. When applied to sense perception and to the Beatific Vision "intuition" signified that both take place without a *species expressa*. This expression "abstractive intuition" belongs indeed to Maritain but the doctrine it conveys comes from St. Thomas and from John of St. Thomas. Aquinas states:

> The intelligible species is to the intellect what the sensible image is to the sense. But the sensible image is not what is perceived but rather that by which the sense perceives. Therefore, the intelligible species is not what is actually understood, but that by which the intellect understands . . . .

And he goes on to say :

> That which is primarily understood is the object of which the species is the likeness . . . . The likeness is of the nature, not of the principles of individuality.[4]

And, more explicitly, John of St. Thomas says:

> For it is not that first the concept is attained and next the object, but in itself immediately the known thing is attained.[5]

We owe Maritain's further clarification of the meaning he attached to the expression "abstractive intuition" to Père Picard, S.J., who questioned the wisdom of it as found in Maritain's work, *Seven Lessons on Being*. Turning to that work I found the following statement: "It follows that the metaphysical intuition of being is an abstractive intuition."[6] The moderns, according to

---

4. Thomas Aquinas, *Summa Theologiae*, I.85.2.
5. John of St. Thomas, *Curs. Theol.* IV, Vives, p. 94, quoted in J. Maritain, *Réflexions*, p. 343.
6. J. Maritain, *A Preface to Metaphysics*, London, Sheed and Ward, 1948, p. 61.

Maritain, substitute object for thing, cutting the object off from existence. Not separating them, Maritain asserts that being is the first object reached by our intellect. Yet Father Picard says:

> The abstractive intuition of M. Maritain, finding its absolute value only in the abstract order, the continuity of the mind's perception between the thinking subject and the real object does not seem sufficiently assured.[7]

To this Maritain replies that he has used the expression because it is a valuable designation of the epistemological doctrine that Thomists defend, and he has used it as a better contrast to certain modern errors of idealism. He is willing to rename the process eidetic or ideating visualization for the sake of those for whom the term "abstraction" is suspect. The new term retains, however, reference to the intelligibility of being. He says:

> I maintain then that the metaphysical intuition of being is an ideating intuition, that is, an intuition producing an idea, and this in a preeminent degree. How could it be otherwise with the pure speculative operation of our human intellect? This intuition is at the summit of eidetic intellectuality. What do I mean by the phrase eidetic visualization, *abstractio*? I mean that the intellect by the very fact that it is spiritual proportions its objects to itself, by elevating them within itself to diverse degrees, increasingly pure, of spirituality and immateriality. It is within itself that it attains reality, stripped of its real existence outside the mind and disclosing, uttering in the mind a content, an interior, an intelligible sound or voice, which can possess only in the mind the conditions of its existence one and universal, an existence of intelligibility in act. If being were the object of a concrete intuition like that of an external sense or of introspection, of an intuition centered upon a reality grasped concretely in its singular existence, philosophy would be compelled to choose, as it gave this intuition an idealist or a realist value, between a pure ontological monism and a pure phenomenalist pluralism.[8]

Being, however, is an analogical term.

Maritain's original expression "abstractive intuition" intended to accent realism over idealism while keeping knowledge the work of the intellect. He speaks of the intellect's natural realism as tending to things under their "essence" aspect. The concept in its intentional role and the object known are indistinguishable. Knowledge is a relation to the real and takes place without changing the object. The relation between the thing known and the soul that knows is a relation of reason, and so knowing does not in any way affect or change the thing known. On the other hand, the relation between the soul that knows and the thing known is a real relation because it places something new in the soul. In abstractions we are still dealing with reality; we are dealing with being as intelligible being. The intellect in act is the intelligible in act. We really do reach the things of the existential world in the world of intelligibility but we do not reach them in their singularity nor in their contingency.

Maritain's concern with establishing a critical realism derives from what he considers to be the epistemological errors of modern philosophers. Kant's

---

7. G. Picard, "Réflexions sur le problème critique," *Archives de philosophie*, XIII, 1, p. 24.
8. Maritain, *A Preface to Metaphysics*, p. 61.

Copernican Revolution—making ideas the measure of things—was preceded by the Cartesian Rebellion—the refusal to start from things, from sensible experience.

When ideas are not drawn from things they can give no knowledge of things. With Descartes the beginning of knowledge is with consciousness, and what is consciously known is the idea of a thing. This idea is an instrumental sign. Thought reaches the idea, reaches itself, not the thing. Then only does the critical problem arise : how do we know that there is anything to which the idea corresponds? With Kant the subject knowing became the formal principle of the act of knowing. The subject constructs objects thanks to the forms of understanding: the unity, the structure, the regulation all come from the mind. It is an autonomous mind, a truthmaking mind. We have seen, however, that Maritain returned to St. Thomas Aquinas and to John of St. Thomas to refute the reification of ideas characteristic of modern idealism.

Referring also to the "intellectual realism" of Blondel, Maritain accuses him of confusing the realism of the will or rational appetite which goes out to the individual reality in its singular and concrete existence, in its very own condition of existing, with the realism of the mind which reaches the nature of the existent itself. He recommended to Blondel the position of "abstractive intuition" whereby the intellect can only become the thing itself by abstraction from the existing conditions and by raising it to an immaterial condition so that it can be known. Blondel is accused of two errors: he has misunderstood the immateriality and interiority proper to intelligence, and he has confused nature and grace in saying that if man were not destined to unitive contemplation he would not be capable of rational life.[9] There is, on the contrary, a formal discontinuity between metaphysical knowledge and divine contemplation. The latter requires the addition of absolutely new formal principles. Blondel's "intellectual realism" is also a confusion between the first and second operation of the mind and is a failure to understand the immediacy of knowledge in the abstractive process. In order to keep God intimate to man, Blondel has thought it necessary to eliminate important distinctions, taking every distinction between two intelligible objects for the affirmation that one actually exists in separation from the other. Although the natural and supernatural orders are distinct, they are not separated from each other.[10]

Although our analysis of abstractive intuition has led us to concentrate on conceptualization, Maritain strongly teaches that the distinction between various concepts should not result in their separation. With St. Thomas, he teaches that truth is in the act of judgment. This act reunites what the act of simple apprehension had divided, identifying the subject with the predicate by means of the verb "to be." By judgment we identify in one same subject two different concepts. The identity between the mind and its object in abstractive

9.   Maritain, *Réflexions sur l'intelligence*, p. 140.
10.   *Ibid.*, pp. 78-141.

intuition precedes the arrival at truth, the conformity between mind and thing when the vital act of affirmation declares "that which is," declares that two objects in concepts, distinct by reason, are the one same thing in extra-mental existence. Our intellectual judgment conforms to an identity in the thing; a mental composition conforms to a real identity. Every judgment, according to Maritain, is a synthesis, but there are various kinds of syntheses. The judgment pertains to existing things. We need the senses not only to derive our ideas from things but also to test our judgments.

Finally, how does Maritain regard cognition? Not as a making, not as a transitive action, but as being other as other. Not only is truth a conformity of the mind with being, but knowledge regarded as quality rather than action, perfects the human being. Being is fundamental to knowledge and to truth. The decadent scholastics and the moderns separated the object known from the thing known. They then had to try to bridge the gap between object and thing.

In his critical examination of knowledge, Maritain has shown that the intellect's natural realism tends to things from the point of view of essence. Knowledge is a relation to the real, and sense knowledge is a prerequisite for the mind's awareness of the first principles. St. Thomas explains it in this way:

> The understanding of first principles is called a natural habit. For it is owing to the very nature of the intellectual soul that man, having once grasped what is a whole and what is a part, should at once perceive that every whole is larger than its part: and in like manner with regard to other such principles. Yet—what is a whole and what is a part— this he cannot know except through the intelligible species which he has received from phantasms: and for this reason the Philosopher at the end of the *Posterior Analytics* shows that knowledge of principles comes to us from the senses. [11]

Maritain notes but does not overemphasize the Idealists' refusal to recognize that ideas originate from sense knowledge. He sees the critical problem which they have bequeathed to philosophers as arising more from misunderstanding the idea as intrumental sign and by confusing the entitative function of the concept with its intentional function. The problem does not arise when the immanent act of understanding both abstracts the essence from its material conditions and immediately attains the object in its immaterial condition as formal sign—thereby reaching the thing as known, its entire specification coming from the object. This philosophical explanation of the meaning of "abstractive intuition" allows Maritain to call himself a critical realist.

---

11. Thomas Aquinas, *Summa Theologiae* I-II.51.1.

Intentionality and the Concept in Jacques Maritain, or The Complexity of Maritain's Doctrine of the Concept. Criticism of Father Roland-Gosselin

DOUGLAS FLIPPEN
Carroll College, Helena, Montana

La doctrine de Maritain sur le concept et l'être intentionnel a fait l'objet de plus d'une critique. Le Père Roland-Gosselin a critiqué l'enseignement de Maritain sur le concept tel que présenté dans Réflexions sur l'intelligence *et* Distinguer pour unir ou Les degrés du savoir. *L'une de ses critiques portait sur le traitement que Maritain réservait à la manière dont le concept est connu dans l'acte même de connaître l'objet par la voie du concept.*

*D'autre part, André Hayen s'attaquait à la manière dont Maritain
semblait détruire l'unité analogique de l'être en accusant le contraste
entre l'être intentionnel et l'être naturel. Ces questions sont reliées
entre elles en autant que la chose qui est connue dans et par le
concept a un être intentionnel plutôt que naturel dans le sujet
connaissant à l'intérieur ou par le moyen du concept.*

*La raison de la présente communication est que ces critiques
ont un fondement réel chez Maritain. Il ne s'ensuit pas cependant
que ces critiques portent. Il subsiste néanmoins un problème, à
savoir, comment interpréter Maritain en ce qui concerne l'inten-
tionnalité et le concept. Sa doctrine n'est pas aussi claire qu'on
le souhaiterait. Analysée sous un aspect, sa doctrine prête flanc
à l'une ou l'autre critique; comprise d'une autre manière, une
manière dont elle n'est pas toujours comprise, elle échappe à la
critique de Roland-Gosselin et de Hayen; bien plus, Maritain est
en accord avec une interprétation littérale de certains textes em-
barrassants de saint Thomas d'Aquin lui-même. Quelle est cette
interprétation? L'être intentionnel de la chose connue dans le
sujet connaissant est identique à l'acte de connaître et n'est qu'une
autre façon de l'envisager, c'est-à-dire, non du point de vue du
sujet connaissant comme cause* efficiente *de son acte de connaître,
mais du point de vue de l'objet connu comme cause* formelle
extrinsèque *de ce même acte. Comme cause formelle extrinsèque,
la chose connue détermine l'acte cognitif en faisant en sorte qu'il
soit l'acte de connaître une chose plutôt qu'une autre et qu'il soit
la chose connue en tant que présente d'une manière représentative
ou intentionnelle dans le sujet connaissant.*

In 1924, Jacques Maritain published his *Réflexions sur l'intelligence et
sur sa vie propre.* In an early section of the work (pp. 50-67 especially)
Maritain, following John of St. Thomas, set forth his teaching on the concept
and on intentionality. In April of the following year Father Roland-Gosselin
reviewed Maritain's work in the *Revue des sciences philosophiques et theo-
logiques.* (pp. 200-203) He had some critical comments concerning Maritain's
doctrine on the concept. In November of that same year, 1925, a Fr. Blanche
defended Maritain's teaching on the concept against Fr. Roland-Gosselin in
a review of the *Réflexions* in the *Bulletin thomiste* (November 1925,
pp. [1]-[7]).

In 1932 the first edition of *Les degrés du savoir* appeared. In chapter 3
(especially section 3) and in the first appendix to the work Maritain repeated